Stage
Management

D0300156

If you can keep your head when all about you are losing theirs and blaming it on you, then you will be a stage manager my friend! (with apologies to Rudyard Kipling)

Stage Management

a gentle art

second edition

Daniel Bond

A & C Black • London
Theatre Arts Books / Routledge • New York

Second edition 1997
First edition 1991
A & C Black (Publishers) Limited
35 Bedford Row, London WC1R 4JH

© 1997, 1991 Daniel Bond

ISBN 0–7136–4551–2

A CIP catalogue record for this book is
available from the British Library.

Published in the U.S.A. in 1998 by
Theatre Arts Books/Routledge
29 West 35 Street, New York, NY 10001

ISBN 0–87830–067–8

CIP available at the Library of Congress.

Front cover photographs left to right:
Nathan Reynard on the lighting board in The Theatre Royal, Newcastle upon Tyne
Jenny Bond marking out in rehearsal
Gary Sparkes in the wings in The Theatre Royal, Newcastle upon Tyne

Typeset in 10¼ on 12pt Photina by
Rowland Phototypesetting Ltd, Bury St Edmunds, Suffolk
Printed and bound in Great Britain by
Lavenham Press Ltd, Suffolk

29342

Contents

For my suns, Matthew J.
Matthew W. E.
Ben
and
BB

I would like to thank the following people for their invaluable help and support in the creation of this book. Many of these people, where possible, have given their services free of charge in support of the charitable spirit of the book.

Jenny Bond
Ian and Josephine Fogden (Illustrations)
The Central School of Speech and Drama
(for permission to reproduce glossary)
The Company and Management of the
1996 Royal Scottish Opera production of *Alceste*
in particular:
Yannis Kikkos – Director & Designer
Gary Sparkes – Stage Manager

Tom Jenkins – Deputy Stage Manager
John La Bouchardiere – Staff Producer
Nathan Reynard – Lighting Board Operator
Michael Wilson – Chief Electrician
John Crawford – Stage Technician
The management and staff of The Theatre Royal,
Newcastle upon Tyne,
Theatre Manager – Peter Orton
Sarah Barker
Jason Barnes
Douglas Cornelissen
Clare Fox
David Lewis
Richard Tierney
Judy Warren
Andy from Gavin Kirkup Studios for photography

Foreword

Having worked in the theatre for over thirty years and also being dyslexic (the BDA is receiving the royalties from *Stage Management – a gentle art*) this book is of particular interest to me. It is a very practical book aimed at helping those who are starting out in the theatre. To lighten the potential frustrations and add to the pleasures the theatre has to offer, Daniel draws out the fundamental production structure. The book also provides checklists and highlights possible pitfalls. The emphasis is quite rightly on the text and those involved in the creation of the play from that text.

Subtleties of communication are the stock and trade of any actor and require precise control of voice and body. There are a myriad of ways in which we physically communicate with each other. Even simple gestures such as a raised eyebrow or a clenched fist can have many different meanings and are wholly dependent on the context in which they are delivered. Similarly, speech is open to interpretation through tone of voice, cadence and timing. It is no wonder therefore that the written word plays such a large part in all our lives. Many people in theatre, education and commerce devote their lives to the interpretation of the written word.

For most of the population reading and writing is an integral part of their lives. If,

therefore, an individual has difficulty with written communication it can form an almost impenetrable barrier to their leading a normal or indeed social life. As the written work so often plays a large role in evaluating a person's ability, those who are not proficient have their whole mental ability brought into question. There are many reasons for having problems with the written word but none so common as dyslexia.

Dyslexia is a specific reading and spelling difficulty. It is particularly related to the written word (alphabetic, numeric or musical notation). It can affect oral language and to some degree organisational skills in general.

Overcoming or, indeed, just coming to terms with dyslexia can be extremely hard. Teachers must learn and develop specialist skills to teach dyslexic children. I am delighted to say that over the past few years awareness of dyslexia has risen dramatically. Sadly, funding is not yet adequate in the already financially overstretched State system, and because of this we must rely on charitable institutions to train teachers, to promote an awareness of the problem.

I am therefore delighted that the royalties from this book have been donated to the British Dyslexia Association.

Happy reading!

Susan Hampshire

Introduction

The intention of this book is to give those with an interest in practising stage management a solid grounding in the skills and understanding needed to function effectively. The many areas in which the stage manager must operate are presented, objectives cited and working procedures discussed – the idea being that if the processes flow smoothly, your own enjoyment of the job will be heightened through your increased efficiency.

When I first started to teach at the Central School of Speech and Drama in London I searched for a concise definition of the stage manager's function in an existing text. Alas, I could find no clear definition in any of the textbooks readily available to the student. And this must, I feel, be indicative of the true nature of stage management. The stage manager has a fluid role, filling the gaps left by others while embracing all angles of the production. The fluidity of the job also derives from the need for the stage management to fit into whatever type of working situation is offered. Taking all these things into account, the best definition I could find was in an American textbook which answered the question 'what does the stage manager do?' with 'the stage manager starts work two weeks before the company begins to rehearse, and finishes work a week after the show closes and during this time he is very busy.' Which is a pretty good way of putting it.

For stage managers to work effectively in the theatre it is important that they have a broad understanding of all aspects of a production: administration, directing, design, set building, stage mechanics, lighting and sound. The one principal component that gives purpose and direction to all these things is, of course, the play.

The play is often somewhat overlooked by a lot of people who purport to be stage managers. These people seem to be so obsessed with the mechanics of staging the play that the play itself is completely obscured. Their time is filled with inanimate objects, timings, and lists. They have no time to talk to actors or listen to the ideas of others. These people are the sort who, not having read the play or looked at the designs, are insistent that a prop they have found is 'just right'. And they have not had time to read the play for it is not on their list of priorities; they do not see the point of reading it, as they have a lot more important things to do. They are heard to say in the bar that they saw the play a couple of years ago and are sure that 'it hasn't changed much since then'. These people are very dangerous and should carry an Arts Council health warning, for they do not realize that the play and the people are the very core of every production.

THE PRODUCTION TREE

I tend to think of a theatrical production as something organic, which is why I use the metaphor 'production tree' to convey my ideas about its development. The play stands as the main trunk – the substance from which all else is derived, with each bough of the tree representing an aspect of the production – lighting, sound, characterization, design, etc. These will grow independently, but require guidance, support, and in some cases pruning, to allow the director to cultivate a well-balanced overall shape. Each bough sprouts lots of twigs – ideas, from which new ideas grow in turn. And eventually the foliage, the carefully planned and created details, will complete the production tree.

This analogy of cultivating a tree is useful throughout the production process. Much forethought is needed to make sure that the resources – finance, space and talent – are neither overstretched nor underdeveloped. The development of the production as a whole is paramount; if one aspect is allowed to grow out of pace with the others it will lack their essential support, something worth remembering for rehearsals.

It is interesting to note that this need to develop the overall shape of a production has led to its being more design oriented. Set designers, costume designers, props designers, sound designers, lighting designers, fight directors, all now have key positions in the theatre. With so many people involved in a production there is an even greater need for excellent communication. Communication of what? Information – information about the ongoing rehearsal process and knowledge of the intentions of all members of the production team. This communicative process must be seen as the first function of good stage management.

Communication is not as simple as it first may seem. For example, the stage manager may need to assess the objectives and requirements of each department, taking account of the staff and resources available. He/she may then need to decide on priorities, plan and structure what action will be taken, and relay this information to all concerned. At another level, it may take a fair amount of skill and organization simply to ensure that a busy actor gets to a fitting on time. Providing the communicative links go further than compiling and distributing detailed notes and diagrams, it means facilitating all aspects of the production from the placing of calls on the call board to cueing actors on stage.

Having stressed the importance of good communication you may well be under the impression that this is the only function of stage management. This, however, is not the case. The demands made of stage management vary from company to company, though the need to provide communication, organization (and be all things to all men and women) are constants. A stage manager should be able to cope with every eventuality, while maintaining a sense of humour and, of course, remaining in control. Stage managers don't panic. The key to the job has to be the word *management*. This is a point that is lost to a great many people in the business of stage management, for they seem to think the *stage* is their main focus. This is really like looking down the wrong end of a telescope, and will lead to all sorts of problems.

Stage management control all the practical aspects of the pre-production period and the performance. With this wide frame of reference in mind, we must examine the attributes of good stage managers. They must be able to organize diverse situations while making certain that they do not lose sight of their original objective. To do this, they must be able to delegate effectively, ensuring that those given a task completely understand both the objective and the process by which they are to achieve it. To motivate others they also need self-confidence and to know that they are fully aware of the work of all concerned in the production.

The people with whom a stage manager is most involved will of course be the performers themselves. The actors represent the sharp end of a performance; when they step up to play a part in the proceedings they have only their talent between them and the audience. To ensure that all the actors' efforts can be directed towards the audience it is essential that they have confidence in all the practical areas of the performance. They need to have confidence that they won't forget their lines and not bump into the furniture – and they must also believe that those around them will ensure that there will be a prompt if they should lose their way in the text and that all the prop dressing will be stuck down in case they do bump into the furniture! If this confidence is instilled in all the actors then it will allow everyone, regardless of their innate ability, to give fully to the production, enabling them to enjoy what they are doing. Enjoyment will give rise to a more relaxed feeling amongst the cast. Many situations in the theatre are far from relaxed, of course, so dispelling the tension is something worth aiming for. To stimulate this feeling of certainty in others, the stage manager must first of all show confidence and endorse this by being reliable. This should be followed through by the stage manager creating and implementing a working structure that relates effectively to the space, the actors and the text. Sensitivity to the nature and style of a production should lead a stage manager to handle people and situations in a variety of different ways.

At this point I would like to take the opportunity to dispel some of the more longstanding myths of the theatre. It is often said by stage management that actors are awkward. This can, in some very few cases, be true but it is usually the result of bad man-management. As I pointed out earlier, actors are indeed at the sharp end of performance, and being in this position can often lead to high anxiety. This sort of tension can manifest itself as awkwardness if it is not diffused through good management. It must also be remembered that actors are in a very competitive marketplace – and if an actor is at the top of the profession it is not surprising that they have become sticklers for detail and are intent on getting what they want.

Another myth that seems to be rife in amateur and student theatre is that theatre is all about working day and night until you drop for practically no money. Sadly, it is still true that the majority of people working in the theatre do not earn good wages, but year by year the situation improves. And theatre should certainly not be about working day and night, for with good management and planning this should not be necessary. (In the past, repertory companies opened a new play every week, while performing an additional two plays. Hours were not limited by union agreements and the role of stage management was not truly acknowledged as it is today.) The overall budget will always dictate staffing levels; and it is important that the work to be done is evaluated in the early stages of pre-production, and the workload judged feasible for the staff available. Working in the theatre, people always want to give 101%, but it is essential for a stage manager to pace both his/her own workload and that of others.

Finally, it is thought by those outside

the theatre that stage management as a profession is always interesting because all the elements of the job are continually changing. It is true to say that the job does change but depending on where you are working the process of change can be very slow. In the West End, stage management can be running the same show with the same people at the same time every night for the same money – for a long time. In this situation, the stage management can only hope to draw pleasure from taking an interest in the play's performance, and a pride in the detail of their prop settings and cueing. It therefore has to be admitted that there are potential moments of ennui in the life of a stage manager.

In writing this book I have endeavoured to illustrate the whole production process from 'soup to nuts', as the Americans say, highlighting the areas that need to be covered by the stage management and related disciplines. To assist with planning and organization I have included a series of checklists within each chapter that can be used as helpful guides for each stage of the production.

1. Backstage Who's Who

Within the theatre structure that exists today the various job titles that people are given will very rarely denote a standard function. In a small fringe theatre company a member of staff may be called a stage manager but will, in truth, be production manager, stage manager, deputy stage manager, assistant stage manager, sound operator and floor sweeper all rolled into one.

In that particular situation the director may well take on board the roles of press officer, producer/director, writer and designer. Theatre in the United Kingdom has always thrived on the flexibility of the men and women working in the field. A theatre may have a stage management team of one or six, but the fundamental stage managerial function will not change – to create organization out of potential chaos. The business maxim 'work expands to fill the time available' can also extend to a job description: 'the job description expands to embrace the job that is to be done'. There are areas of responsibility which do come with a job but the detail relating to them must be developed and agreed upon by the production team. Nothing in this industry is written in stone, for the requirements of every production are different.

Bearing this in mind, I have drawn up a list of job titles and the perceived function of each. These may well be adapted to fit the circumstances presented.

Producer

Producers are usually found in the commercial sector of the theatre. Producers and production companies are the people who conceive the idea of performing a certain text with certain actors in a certain place. The chosen place, i.e. the theatre, will, of course, need to be sufficiently large to recoup the projected outgoings and, of course, make a profit. The producer or production company will then take this package to possible investors, known as 'angels' or backers. Very often investment in a production may be dependent on their having secured the services of a particular actor or director. Once the producer has financial guarantees of investment the process of production will commence.

During production, the producer will continually liaise with the director and the designer to ensure, at least in part, that the original concept has not been lost. The producer is also responsible for the clearance of copyright, commissioning of publicity, booking of performers, staff and venue. Having conceived the idea of performing a play, the producer must to a certain extent then stand back from the process of production and allow those who have been employed to do the job, do it.

Director

In the British subsidized theatre a director will be chosen from a number of applicants by the Board of Governors of the theatre. The Board of Governors are appointed to ensure the good use of public funds, and will therefore choose the director on the basis of his or her approach to the arts and specific intentions for the theatre in question. Most British regional subsidized theatres give their directors a three year contract, which in many cases is often renewed.

In a regional repertory theatre the director will work hand in hand with a general manager; together they will estimate the production, staff and building costs.

In the commercial theatre a director will be called in by a producing management. The director will be required to deal with all aspects of the play's production but he/she will in many cases not have a significant part in the advertising or overall management of the production.

In both commercial and subsidized theatre a director's principal role is to direct the performances of actors and develop all aspects of the play to create a cohesive whole.

Designer

Design is, and has always been, an integral part of any production. A designer's responsibilites cover all the visual elements of a production, including the acting space, props and lighting. The theatre designer is not entirely concerned with aesthetics, for he must also be fully aware of the practicalities of that which he creates. For example, a steep raked stage may have tremendous appeal visually, but a designer cannot incorporate it into a design without first recognizing and dealing with the practical problems this concept will present. A truly responsible designer will pay as much attention to the detail of a production as he does to the overall concept, knowing that the two are inexorably linked.

The designer will work with the director and lighting designer to create conceptual links and in practical issues will liaise with the production manager and stage manager. The production budget will be ever-present in all these conversations, not necessarily representing a constraint but being used more as a working guideline.

A designer will invariably create a scale model of the proposed design to accompany the plans and elevations of the stage.

Production Manager

Production managers are found in both commercial and subsidized theatres. In fringe theatre the function of a production manager is very often embraced by the stage manager. The production manager's job is to oversee the overall cost effectiveness and technical planning of a production. In many cases their involvement may well start before that of a stage manager.

Production managers should be well versed in all the technical aspects of production, scenery construction, costume, lighting, sound and, of course, stage management. Their principal function is to advise and supervise technically the work of others and contain costs while adhering to the schedule that was originally devised. It is their partial responsibility to see that staff fulfil their contractual obligations. The production manager will not usually be involved during the performance, other than to view the final show from the auditorium and give notes to the various departments concerned during the final stages of production.

Company Stage Manager

Company stage managers are sometimes found in large regional repertory companies but this is exceptional – they are usually employed in commercial and West End theatre, and are responsible for the overall running of a production in performance. In pre-production they will be responsible for the employing of production staff and the co-ordination of the various departments involved in the production. In performance they have sole responsibility for the running of the show. This includes the payment of staff and in some cases the documentation and monitoring of box office receipts. A company manager should be conversant with all contractual matters concerning the performers, staff, and the venue itself ensuring that contractual conditions are adhered to on both sides at all times. In short, in performance their word is law. They will additionally in many cases be required to take understudy rehearsals, directing the action as indicated in the prompt copy.

Resident Stage Manager

Theatrical touring venues will all have a resident stage manager who is responsible for the technical liaison and show staffing for any production that enters the theatre's doors. If you are touring you must ensure that you form a solid working relationship with this person, who has the power to make your life a pleasure or a pain. This position is very often held by someone who has been with the theatre for a long, long time, who will claim to have seen and done it all and they often have. Stimulating enthusiasm in these individuals may seem a mountainous task but persist, for they usually do more than they tell you they will!

Stage Manager

The stage managerial function is undoubtedly the most fluid of all the theatrical disciplines. The role of a stage manager in the commercial theatre is usually undertaken by the company manager with certain aspects of the job being delegated to the resident stage manager of the venue where the performance is to take place.

In subsidized regional theatres the role of stage manager is much more clearly defined. He/she works directly to the production manager and is responsible for running of rehearsals, finding props and servicing the shows in performance. Generally the stage management team will cover these responsiblities, but sometimes a sole stage manager will have to handle everything – it has been known to happen.

Deputy Stage Manager

The deputy stage manager is quite often the title given to the member of the stage management team who acts as the prompter and cuer in rehearsal and performance. This is a specific function and there are a lot of people in the commercial theatre who have made this particular job their life. However, working 'on the book' in rehearsal is not always given to the DSM. In some theatre structures it is done by the stage manager and in others by the assistant stage manager. Whatever the situation, a DSM should always be capable of deputizing for the stage manager.

Working closely with directors and actors requires particular skills, and a well-balanced mixture of assertiveness and deference.

Assistant Stage Manager

The assistant stage manager's principal function is to assist with the ongoing requirements of rehearsal and performance. This usually means taking responsibility for the finding, servicing and setting of props, but the role of the ASM may be extended depending on the working environment. It can include liaison with technical departments, actors and management, but on the other hand it can also embrace more mundane things, such as making tea and mopping the stage. An ASM is directly responsible to the stage manager and to the deputy stage manager in his/her absence.

Stage Crew

Stage crew in British regional repertory theatres are very often sourced from people in other professions who have an interest in theatre or in making additional money. In most cases it is the latter, but occasionally it can be both. A stage crew of this sort requires very careful handling and organization. Because the crew members don't rely solely on the money they earn from working in the theatre they can develop a rather flippant attitude to the whole process.

Stage crew in the London's West End tend, on the whole, to work in theatre as a profession. There are a number of personalities in the West End who have been moving scenery and furniture for years. The interest, enthusiasm and experience of these people can add a lot to the production process. In some instances stage crew may be allocated specifically to electrical duties, in which case they are called stage electricians.

When a member of a theatre's stage crew is given work totally relating to the production in performance they are given the title showman. This has, I believe, not yet been adapted to showperson, even though there are a large number of women working in this area.

Master Carpenters

The name Master Carpenter can often be given to the resident stage managers of touring venues. In a normal situation, however, the master carpenter would be found running the scenic workshop. The master carpenter must be treated with care as you can be sure that he/she has been mistreated by management and production staff alike during the course of his/her career. This is primarily due to the position not being sufficiently well acknowledged as one of management and technical expertise.

Flyman

A head flyman is the person given responsibility in the theatre for keeping control of the fly floors in fit-up, rehearsal and performance. This requires a careful eye for detail and an ability to focus on an operation, very often after hours of waiting. A lack of concentration on the fly floor while operating a cue could potentially cause a disaster on stage. The head flyman or showman is directly responsible to the stage manager.

Wardrobe Master/Mistress

A wardrobe master/mistress is responsible for the hiring and making of all the costumes used in a production and for their subsequent upkeep in performance. It is a job which also requires a great deal of tact and care when dealing with the practical and emotional needs of actors. The wardrobe master/mistress must also liaise with technical departments such as sound over the positioning of radio microphones. For some productions a wig mistress/master will be taken on to ensure the wigs are properly dressed for each performance, but this task may well be left to the person running the wardrobe department.

Finally, there will be the hiring and organizing of cutters, machinists and, of course, dressers.

Dressers

A dresser's work is principally in performance and related rehearsals. Where a performance requires quick changes to be made or has a large chorus a dresser may well be employed to ensure that costume changes are effected as smoothly and calmly as possible.

When a quick change has to be made, the dresser will first ensure that everything which is needed is taken to the quick change area, where all the pieces of the costume should be laid out in exactly the same way as in rehearsal. The dresser may be required to help an actor with zips, buttons, shoes, socks, corsets, wigs, hats, ties and jewellery. While this happens the dresser must ensure that the actor is made to feel calm and relaxed and able to continue effectively with the performance.

Principal stars may often have a preferred dresser who tends to work with them. Such dressers often extend their duties to include the complete organization of that star while he/she is in the theatre.

Lighting Designer

As it is such an integral part of the performance, lighting design may well be included in the early conceptual discussions of a production team – indeed it should be. A lighting designer must be capable of manipulating the available technical facilities to produce a result that is in keeping with the show as conceived by the director and designer. This is not to say that a lighting designer only creates on demand, for there are many ways of devising an effect. He/she creates a structured format by combining the uses of colour with the angle and intensity of the lanterns.

After discussion with the designer and director and attendance at rehearsals, the lighting designer will produce a detailed lighting design. This takes the form of a plan of the stage and auditorium showing the position of each lantern to be used and the colour, if any, to be inserted in the lantern. From this plan the lanterns will be rigged in the initial stages of the production rig. Once in position they will be focused by the lighting designer so that they cover the area of the stage allocated to them.

During the lighting session and performance the designer will assign a crew member to operate the lighting board. The chief electrician will ensure the smooth running of the show as plotted by the lighting designer. Once the play is in performance the designer will often move on to another production.

Lighting Crew

The lighting crew are a specialist team of technicians who are able to follow through the design drawn up by the lighting designer: this will involve rigging lanterns and cables, cutting colour, plugging up dimmer racks and operating lighting boards and follow spots.

Sound Designer

This is a position that has only relatively recently been acknowledged by the theatre at large. Like the lighting designer, sound designers can very often benefit from being involved with the production at an early stage. In the case of a musical they must select the required microphones, mixers, amplifiers and speakers to ensure effective sound coverage in both the auditorium and on stage. Sound designers will also be involved in the creation/selection of sound effects and backing tracks.

Front of House Manager

The front of house manager is usually engaged by the general manager of the theatre or venue. FOH managers do not usually move from theatre to theatre with the production for they are regarded as permanent members of staff. The FOH manager will be responsible for the running of the box office and tallying of receipts, sometimes via a box office manager. The front of house area technically stops at the pass door of a proscenium arch theatre, which means that the FOH manager is also responsible for the auditorium itself, toilets, fire exits, bars and front of house display. The stage/company manager will need to liaise with the front of house manager over complimentary tickets, show timings, programmes, understudies and box office receipts.

Any stage/company manager should ensure a good working relationship with the front of house manager who, although it may not seem so at first glance, is holding an absolutely essential management position in the theatre structure. At Christmas in the pantomime season in the United Kingdom the stage/company manager may think that they have got the thin end of the wedge when they must delay the start of a performance for some unavoidable reason. At this point they should spare a thought for the FOH Manager who has 800 impatient children to cope with, who do you think has the best deal?

Stage Doorman/Woman

In most theatres that have a stage door it is usual for a person to be employed to sit at the stage door while the production is in process and monitor the comings and goings. These tend to be personalities who have held the position for some years, whose attentiveness can prove to be equally as useful as their knowledge of the locale. Stage doormen/women will often be responsible for issuing dressing room keys and logging staff and performers in and out. Organisation of taxis, distribution of mail and football results can all fall to the person at the stage door. Other than the stage management team they are the only other department (if it may be called such) that has access to the back stage tannoy. This is primarily for calling people to the stage door when they have visitors or a phone call. They come into their own when dealing with ardent fans and vagrants, both of whom have a tendency to appear at stage doors – and an ability to recognize the difference is essential!

2. *The Theatre*

When I first started out in the theatre at the age of sixteen I worked with a street theatre group, for whom there was no proscenium arch, no wings and no gods (but for the heavens that opened often enough). From this I moved to a studio theatre and finally on to my first grown-up (as I then thought) proscenium arch theatre. There I learnt the basics of my theatre vocabulary, sometimes the hard way.

On my first day I was put through the mill. Sent to the flys to watch the hemps and counterweights being flown in and out as part of a fit-up, I continually found myself in the wrong place at the wrong time. Bridles, drifts and deads were discussed. Eventually bored with having the back of his head drilled with my stare, the head flyman gave me a job to do, saying 'Go and ask Frank if he's got any long weights left'. Thinking this might have something to do with counterweight equipment, but not really knowing and very anxious not to show my ignorance, I nervously descended the Jacob's ladder (which as it involved looking down was a different ball game to going up). On arrival at the stage floor I sought out the elusive stage manager, Frank. He, when asked, duly told me to wait a moment while he got a couple of other things sorted out. After about ten minutes or so of watching a totally disinterested Frank, I finally got it – 'A long wait!' I mounted the Jacob's ladder with renewed gusto. On arrival I was greeted with a bunch of flymen clapping their hands and holding their stomachs, having been hardly able to contain themselves as they watched from above. I'd been set up – the latest in a long line of unsuspecting fall guys, no doubt! We learn something new every day . . . Other mythical equipment that you might watch out for are the likes of 'keys to the grid', 'sky hooks' and 'left handed hammers'.

In an attempt to prevent the readers of this book from similar misunderstandings of technical jargon, this chapter describes and names the different parts of a theatre. No theatre is exactly the same as another,

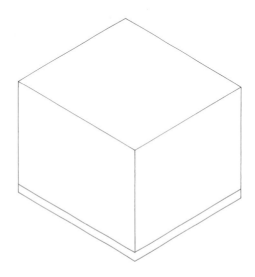

2.1 The theatre

though they tend to contain similar elements. To identify all of these variations would be an endless task, of benefit to no-one. I have therefore chosen to illustrate a traditional proscenium arch theatre as found all over the world, which should provide a useful basis for understanding. The concepts and vocabulary described here can be used in any working situation, be it a studio, theatre, open-air venue or any untraditional performance space. In whatever capacity we may find ourselves working the need to communicate with all those in the theatre is paramount. As with any industry, without the vocabulary we are restricted to 'the thingumajig' and 'you know, over there' which is hardly conducive to safe or rapid working.

The Theatre

To identify the different areas of the stage floor a grid format is very often used to denote the upstage, centrestage and downstage areas (see fig 2:2). These positions are used when giving instructions for the positioning of scenery, props and lighting. For the purposes of logging actors' moves in the prompt script a version of this grid is applied to the acting area.

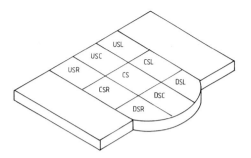

2.2 The stage floor

The stage surface may contain rectangular lifts positioned across the stage which can be used to move scenery into position from the understage area. Referred to as bridge lifts, they are found in a number of large theatres and opera houses, quite often incorporated into a revolve.

There is often a need both within a performance and for practical storage reasons to have access to the understage area. Lift-out sections of stage are good for storage but have little use as an inter-performance device, so many theatres also incorporate a traditional grave trap that is operated from the understage area. This allows a section of stage to be slid back under the stage surface; then by means of a counter-weight winch or hydraulic system another section of stage of the same size can be

USR	Upstage right	USOP	Upstage opposite prompt
USC	Upstage centre	USC	Upstage centre
USL	Upstage left	USPS	Upstage prompt side
CSR	Centrestage right	CSOP	Centrestage opposite prompt
CS	Centrestage	CS	Centrestage
CSL	Centrestage left	CSPS	Centrestage prompt side
DSR	Downstage right	DSOP	Downstage opposite prompt
DSC	Downstage centre	DSC	Downstage centre
DSL	Downstage left	DSPS	Downstage prompt side

moved or partly moved up to fit into the gap left by the removed section.

Dip traps and cloth traps are the only other two traps to be found on the stage surface. Dips are shallow traps that conceal power supplies and technical service points. Cloth traps are found at the front of a lot of opera stages and are used to jam the leading edges of floor cloths prior to their being stretched up stage.

Most theatres were built or have been modernized to deal with the prospect of the theatre catching fire. A glass section of roof, known as the lantern, is positioned above the fly tower, and opens in case of fire: its release is either automatic (in the presence of heat) or will be effected by the heat of the fire breaking the glass. This creates an updraught, drawing the fire up the flytower like a chimney away from the rest of the building. On the auditorium side of the flytower a fire wall is constructed running the full height of the building and dividing the flytower from the void above the auditorium. There are only two gaps in this wall, one somewhat bigger than the other, and they are the proscenium arch and the pass door. The proscenium arch will in the event of fire be sealed by the safety curtain (the iron) and the pass door should be left closed at all times with restricted access to staff. The flytower itself

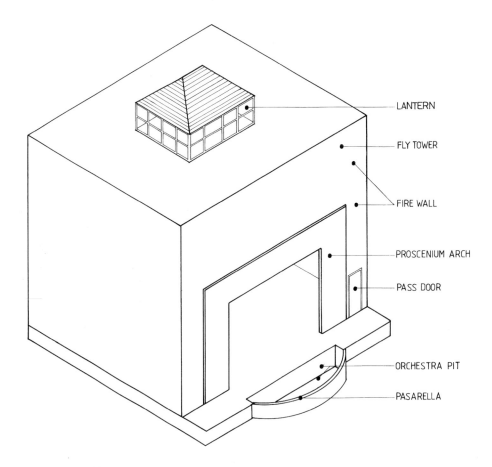

LANTERN

FLY TOWER

FIRE WALL

PROSCENIUM ARCH

PASS DOOR

ORCHESTRA PIT

PASARELLA

2.3 The stage walls

is constructed to contain all the rigging equipment required to lift and hold large weights above the stage.

The forestage is the area that protrudes in front of the line of the proscenium arch. In front of this may often be found a 'D' lift, a section of stage shaped like a D, on hydraulic cylinders, that can be raised or lowered to form an extension to the forestage or descend to create an orchestra pit. The rail that runs round the outside of the orchestra pit is sometimes referred to as the pasarella.

The iron or safety curtain (known in US/Europe as the fire curtain) forms a giant draught excluder between the audi- torium and the stage. Its effectiveness was proven in 1989 when the auditorium of the Savoy Theatre, London was gutted with fire but the backstage area remained intact. This was entirely due to the iron being in place.

To extinguish flame and assist with cooling the iron has above it a drencher pipe. When the iron is released the drencher pipe sprays water over it. The releases for both iron and drencher pipe can be found in the stage left wing (prompt side) of most theatres.

Flying systems vary from theatre to theatre but the fundamentals are the same. Hemp (rope) systems are usually

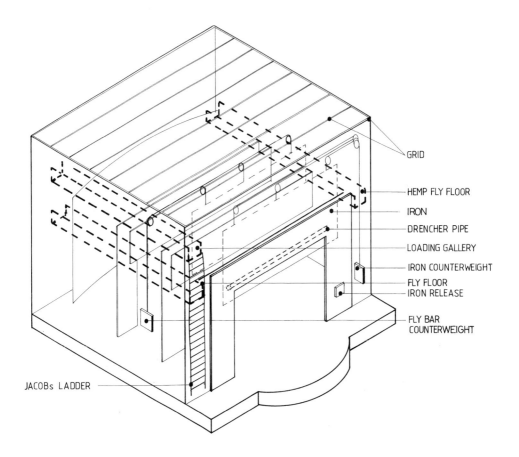

2.4 *(a) The flying systems*

operated from the fly floor, a gallery situated approximately half way between stage floor and grid running up and down stage. Hemp systems operate using three lines: long, centre, short and are named so depending on the position of the fly floor from which they are operated. The lines go over a head pulley and out to one of three pulley blocks attached to the grid that divert the lines down to a steel hollow bar. To assist with the even distribution of weight an additional piece of rope can be inserted called a bridle, which looks like an inverted Y above the bar. The total distance that a flying bar can be moved from stage floor to knots (touching pulley blocks in the case of a hemp set) is referred to as the drift.

Hemps can be difficult to work with for when a piece of scenery or a drape is attached to a bar which has to be pulled out the operators have to haul three ropes together by bunching them. As this is awkward and heavy there should be at least three operators to each set when pulling a loaded bar out, two to pull the ropes out, hand over hand, and one to hold the rope round the cleat to take in the slack and tie off when the move is complete. Each set of three lines has two cleats allocated to it, the bottom cleat to tie the ropes off at the lower operational position and the top cleat to tie the ropes off at the upper operational position. These positions are called the 'deads'. Prior to setting the 'deads' the bar must be levelled at the bottom dead. To do this, the operators must identify the long, centre and short, which is made possible by means of colour coded tapes or coloured strands twisted into the fabric of the rope. Using this method the stage manager on the floor will instruct the operators to 'pull up on the long or down on the short' until the bar is level. The dead cannot be deemed to be set until the operators have bunched the ropes, tied off and stood clear of the cleat. Prior to confirming a 'dead' it can help to 'bounce' each line. This is a process whereby each line is pulled out a short way and released, which ensures that any slack in the knot and the rope itself is released.

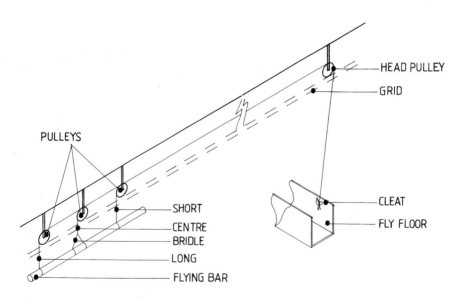

2.4 (b) Hemp pulley system

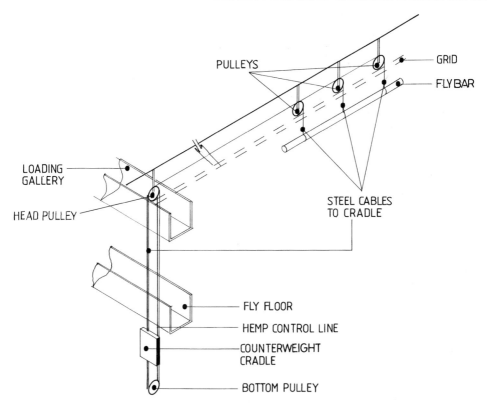

2.4 *(c) Counterweight pulley system*

If a single rope operated from the fly floor is specifically positioned in the grid to pick up a piece of scenery, cyc or boom it is referred to as a spot line. If a flying bar is tied off the grid on a fixed length of rope it is referred to as a dead line since it has a fixed drop.

Hemp can be affected by dry and damp weather and the process of checking and redeading hemps must be done every day.

Counterweight systems operate in a similar way but without the perspiration. Instead of rope, the long, centre and short going out to the bar are steel cables. The cables are attached to the bar and run back to the fly floor via a series of pulleys. At the fly floor end the cables are attached to a weights cradle. By putting weights in the cradle relative to the weight on the bar in a ratio of one to one (with a single purchase system) and two to one (with a double purchase system), the weight on the bar can be counterbalanced by the weight in the cradle.

The movement of the counterweight cradle and hence the bar is determined by the movement of a control line that forms an endless loop; it is attached to the top of the cradle, going over a head pulley and down to a bottom pulley. From this point it is attached to the bottom of the cradle. The movement of the cradle is restricted by the greased slider in which it moves up and down. The drift of a counterweight bar is restricted by the movement of the cradle in the slider and most counterweight bars will not travel all the way to the stage floor. This is not a problem with single purchase systems but can lead to problems with double purchase counterweights. The control line can be marked with tape to indicate the operational deads and be locked off by means of a brake on the control line.

The operation of a counterweight system relies on the weight on the bar being evenly balanced with the weight in the cradle. An imbalance can prove dangerous, for the control line brakes are not designed to take great strains with total safety. When picking up a piece of scenery the bar is lowered to the stage floor and the cradle rises to the loading gallery level where the majority of the weights are stored, and the cradle is initially loaded

when the bar is at stage level. The drape or piece of scenery is attached to the bar, and at this point a certain amount of weight can be put into the cradle – usually 60 and 30lb (27 and 13½ kilos) weights are available. It is important, however, not to put too much in the cradle at this stage. If the cradle is too heavy and the weight on the bar (at this point) is not yet taking effect due to the bar being at stage level, the weight in the cradle may snatch the control line from the operator's hand, and cause the bar to rise rapidly and uncontrollably. To help with this situation weights can be added at the fly floor level to even out the weight in the cradle against the weight on the bar. Nothing

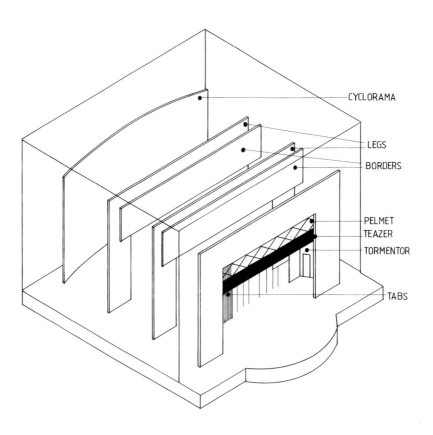

CYCLORAMA

LEGS

BORDERS

PELMET
TEAZER

TORMENTOR

TABS

2.5 Dressing the proscenium

beats an experienced eye when judging the weight of a piece of scenery and nothing is worse or more dangerous than inexperience in this area.

Quite often pieces of scenery have to be flown close together. To allow one piece to be flown past another those round it have to be moved up or down stage. The method usually employed is a breast line. This is a rope that is stretched between the fly rails on the fly floors stage left and stage right and pulled tightly so as to pull a piece of scenery out of the way. Another method that can be used to create the same effect is 'brailing'. A brail is a line attached to the ends of a flying bar and tied off on the fly floor. The disadvantage of brail lines is that if the bar is flown to the grid the lines must be released. For this reason they are more often used for static bars. The running plot for the flys of a big show well may include a number of brail or breast line movements during the course of the performance.

The fly bar may well be a fixed length but when a border is hung it may need extending to the fly floor. This is done by inserting a smaller bore pipe inside the flying bar with sufficient excess remaining inside the bar to pull it out beyond the end of the pipe.

Some very modern theatres are equipped with a large number of individual electric hoists that can be linked in any order to operate in unison. This means there is the potential to pick up oddly shaped scenery – but alas, the flytower still remains the same shape.

The pelmet in a theatre usually has one single function, to cover the bottom of the iron that sticks out below the line of the proscenium arch (see fig. 2:5). This happens because of the sheer size of the iron, combined with the lack of room in the fly tower to accommodate it. The iron obviously has to be the size it is to fulfil its func-

tion as a fire block. Hanging inside the proscenium arch the pelmet looks like and indeed functions as a pelmet, for directly up stage of the iron hang the front curtains, known as the tabs. These are usually on a counterweight system operated from the fly floor, though they can also be operated from the stage floor.

Cycloramas are often created in theatres in a number of ways – one way of doing it has been to construct a large brick and plaster edifice in the furthest upstage position. A classic example of this used to be found at Glyndebourne Opera in the south of England. In the contemporary theatre the need for cycloramas as a permanent structure has somewhat waned. The most common method of creating a 'cyc', as they are called, is to stretch a shark's tooth gauze a minimum distance (40cm or 16 inches) in front of a plain white cloth. When lit this gives a depth that cannot easily be created when using a single surface.

The teaser, tormenter, legs and borders all combine to create the traditional masked black box from which grow so many theatre concepts. All these items are defined and described in detail in the section called 'masking' on page 30 of this chapter.

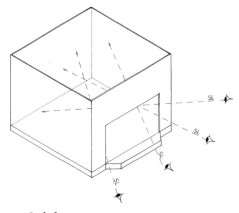

2.7 Sightlines

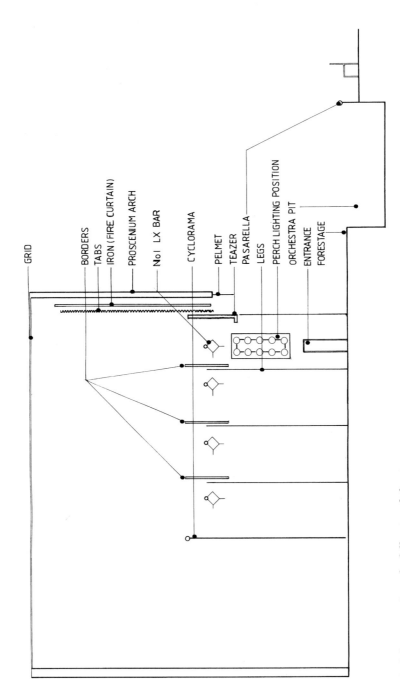

GRID

BORDERS
TABS
IRON (FIRE CURTAIN)
PROSCENIUM ARCH
No I LX BAR
CYCLORAMA
PELMET
TEAZER
PASARELLA
LEGS
PERCH LIGHTING POSITION
ORCHESTRA PIT
ENTRANCE
FORESTAGE

2.6 Cross-section of a fully rigged theatre

The line of vision (sightlines) for each member of the audience from the auditorium to the stage needs to be taken into account, both at the design stage and as the play progresses through rehearsal (see fig. 2:7). The designer and the director will initially work together to produce a stage set that in visual and practical terms maximizes the potential of the auditorium for the benefit of the play. During this process the designer will be working towards combining the visual elements to create an aesthetic whole. The director, too has the visual aspect in mind, and is also seeking to create a physical space that will enhance the development of action and text. And with all this going on everyone has to be certain that a good percentage of the audience can see the action you are staging. This means that the line of vision from all of the extremes of the auditorium has to be examined and evaluated, and the director and designer between them arrive at a compromise. The designer must take on board the staging mechanics just as the director must be equally aware of the lines of sight for each potential member of the audience. For both parties, concept development will mean a continued reappraisal of both the text and the performance space, with an overriding awareness of costs.

To establish lines of sight it is necessary to draw up a plan and elevation/section of both the stage and the auditorium. This allows the line of sight to be identified from the extreme seating positions, both horizontally (lateral) and vertically. These lines of sight from the auditorium to the stage are referred to as the 'sightlines'.

When drawing a 'sightline' a dashed line is used with SL marked on top of the line. An arrowhead is only used when the sightline drawn meets with a piece of scenery, masking or even the theatre structure and the line of sight is interrupted (see fig. 2:8(a) and (b)). The extreme lines of sight from the gallery, stage boxes and front of stalls are marked in, as it is assumed that if these are covered all other lines of sight will be acceptable. This is not always the case and a wary eye (so to speak) should be kept on other seating positions relative to entrances and lighting positions. Sightlines will dictate the positioning of masking, lighting equipment, door backings, furniture and, of course, scenery. The director will have a continual battle with sightlines as the play is blocked in rehearsal and actors are given positions relative to audience and scenery. Even the angle of a hat will be affected by sightlines – can those in the gallery see the actor's face? (This problem would also pose the following questions: would the character wear such a hat at such an angle; how will the lighting designer light the actor's face; do we need to see the actor's face at this point? All these points indicate that potential problems are best identified

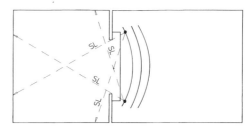

2.8 (a) Theatre plan showing sightlines from front row of stalls

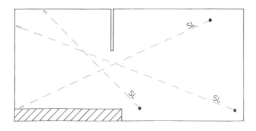

2.8 (b) Theatre section showing sightlines from front and back of stalls and balcony

at an early stage, something discussed continually throughout the book.

In studio theatre in the round, sight-lines take on a new importance as every aspect of the action has (in some way) to work for each member of the audience, as with traverse staging. In these cases, the visual background to the action is very often the audience and sightline problems are found with furniture, actors and lights (in the eyes). Studio sightlines can be tricky and they can often give rise to unplanned sightlines such as backstage staff, on entrances and exits. I will leave you with a simple and yet exact statement I saw pinned up on a backstage wing flat: 'If you can see them, they can see you.' This can be alleviated by the marks of lines of sight on the floor of the offstage area at each entrance.

MASKING

The masking of all areas of the stage with black material is commonplace in the theatre as we know it. It is, however, by no means a standard requirement. The play itself, and its interpretation by the director and designer will determine what the audience will finally see. For the staging of an Agatha Christie it is practically essential to mask the offstage area. If the murderer is seen loitering by a door prior to an entrance the element of surprise would be somewhat diminished. On the other hand the staging of a musical may be greatly enhanced by including the lights and rigging as part of the visuals. If included they will have to be designed into the overall look of the piece, which may require additional lighting booms, lanterns or battens that do not serve a real technical function but heighten the visual effect. These are two extremes – but we must acknowledge

that we no longer work in a theatre where all the technical aspects of a per-formance have to be continually covered up. It is, for example, quite common to see the lanterns top lighting the stage from the flys. We should, however, always remain in control of that which the audience sees.

The three types of material most com-monly used for masking are: wool serge, Bolton twill and velour. Though other colours are widely used in variety shows, black is most commonly used in the the-atre. Black comes in many shades and care should be taken to ensure that there is continuity of colour and density. Bolton twill is the most unsatisfactory form of black masking, as it does not hang well and unless heavily lined allows light through from backstage. Velour has advantages, for a thick pile velour can pro-vide a very dense black. Unfortunately velour has the same disadvantage as Bolton twill in respect of fire proofing (see fire appendix p. 119). Wool serge, on the other hand, is inherently fireproof and provides a dense black backdrop. When any material is to be used on a 'wing flat' it must be stretched, and to ensure that it does not become translucent with stretch-ing it should be backed with a canvas that has been painted black. A generic term for all black masking is 'blacks'.

The classic down stage masking format that is to be found in a number of theatres as a semi-permanent structure is formed by the creation of a false black proscenium arch. This is placed in the same position as the proscenium, one metre (3¼ft) upstage of the main proscenium arch. Downstage to the left and right the vertical masking goes off at an angle to join with the back of the proscenium. These vertical flats are called the 'tormenters' and very often they have small arch entrances cut into them with small curtain tracks behind. At a higher level vertical slots are cut for lighting (referred to as 'perches') that allow the downstage area to be cross lit. Should there be a traditional front cloth scene change the front cloth would be dropped just upstage of the false proscenium and the actors would gain entrance to the downstage area via the

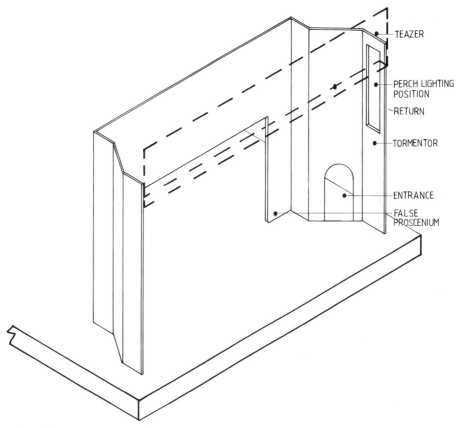

2.9 (a) False proscenium masking

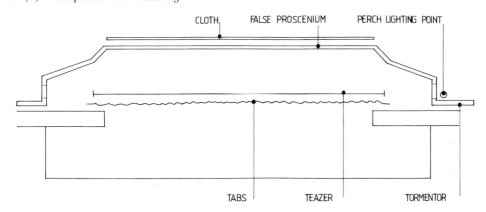

2.9 (b) Plan of proscenium masking

arches in the tormenters. The lighting for this scene would come from FOH with perches to the left and right of the stage plus light from the number one bar usually positioned directly upstage of the 'teaser'. The teaser is in turn directly upstage of the tabs. The teaser forms a black insert to the proscenium that runs horizontally, allowing the proscenium height to be varied. This piece of masking is usually rigid in structure and 'L' shaped in section, the thin flat on the bottom upstage edge is known as a return. This masks the number one Lx bar from the front stalls.

On stage masking is dealt with in two distinct areas, directly related to the horizontal and vertical planes of vision which comprise the sightlines (see fig 2:9(a) and (b)). Vertical side stage masking is used to mask off the wings and comes in two forms, 'legs' and 'wing' flats.

Legs (fig 2:10(a)) can be hung from steel or aluminium tubes (called 'barrels') above the stage which in turn may be attached to a flying system. Legs are attached to the barrel by means of ties. When tying a leg on to a barrel it can be more effective to

turn the onstage edge back on itself by two ties, giving a cleaner edge. Most legs are gathered into folds to increase the density of the black and have chain sewn into the hems. When space is restricted legs can be very useful, as they are eaily drawn to one side to allow for the movement of scenery. When a large scene change is being carried out in a a theatre with a flying system the legs can be flown out to allow free movement of scenery and dropped back in place at the end of the change.

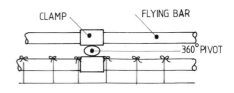

2.10 (b) Underslung leg on 360° pivot

Legs by their very nature, run off/on stage in line with the proscenium arch and if attached directly to a flying bar they cannot be angled. It is possible through the use of a swivel clamp (designed for the job) to under sling another bar which has a centrally positioned swivel on to which the leg is tied (fig 2:10(b)). This allows the leg to be positioned at an angle to the stage, but it will restrict the bars movement, making it virtually impossible to fly the bar in question. For this reason this type of set up is more commonly found in non-flying theatres.

A number of legs may be attached to a tab track, and when overlapped can form a complete wall of black; this can be drawn open and closed like a large pair of curtains by means of a drawrope positioned to one side of the stage. More often than not these 'travellers' are specially made in two large panels and attached to the bobbins on the track with spring clips.

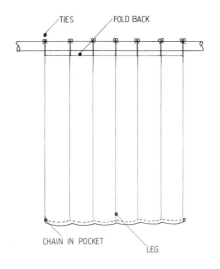

2.10 (a) Hanging a leg

The 'drop' of the legs (the distance from ties to the hem chain) should be well in excess of the height of the proscenium

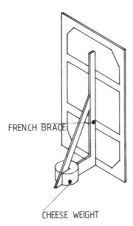

FRENCH BRACE

CHEESE WEIGHT

2.10 (c) French brace

opening to allow the borders to cover the barrel from which they are hung.

Wing flats are another alternative to vertical masking. They too must be tall enough

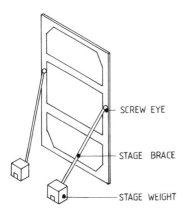

SCREW EYE

STAGE BRACE

STAGE WEIGHT

2.10 (d) Weights and braces

to run the full height of the proscenium opening while being wide enough to have an effect. Wing flats are very often used in pairs so that one flat or leg will run on and

offstage while the other runs up and downstage. Given the need for these to be so tall they also require a great deal of support. French braces (fig 2:10(c)), are very often used in conjunction with cheese weights on the base; these are specially constructed braces that run almost the full height of the flat.

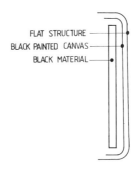

FLAT STRUCTURE

BLACK PAINTED CANVAS

BLACK MATERIAL

2.10 (e) Cladding a masking flat

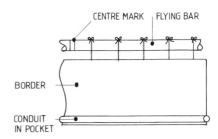

CENTRE MARK   FLYING BAR

BORDER

CONDUIT
IN POCKET

2.10 (f) Hanging a border (with conduit pocket)

Alternatively, adjustable stage braces (fig 2:10(d)) can be used in conjunction with screw eyes in the flat and stage weights or stage screws to hold the foot of the brace firmly on the floor.

To mask horizontally, large panels of black material are used similar to the teaser but without a rigid structure. These 'borders' can be given a clean hard edge by inserting a small bore tube into the conduit pocket on the lower edge (fig 2:10(f)). If used in a theatre with flys the height of these borders can be adjusted to suit the staging and sightlines. In a theatre with a fixed low ceiling the borders are very often made a specific depth to ensure there is sufficient masking from the front of the stalls.

Having identified the forms of masking that are now available to us we can now

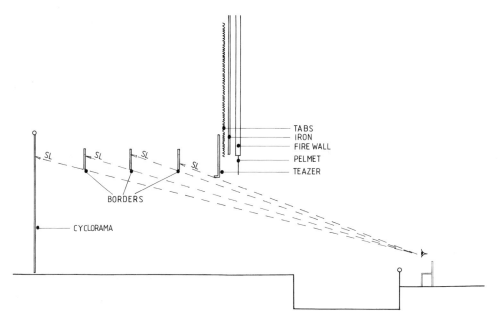

2.11 (a) Plan showing borders masking the stage

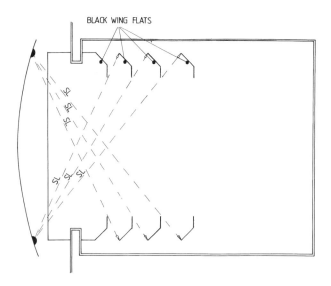

2.11 (b) Section showing wing flats masking the stage

combine these with our understanding of theatre sightlines to create what is commonly known as a 'black box'. This means to all intents and purposes, that wherever a member of the audience sits they will be looking at a black box. This is a very common format for dance, with the gap between the legs/masking flats used for entrances and exits, with positions provided for lighting booms than can cross light the stage.

It must at this point be noted that there has to be an element of compromise with regard to the masking process. With so many wraparound auditoriums in existence that have boxes and seats very close to the stage it is sometimes impossible to cover all sightlines without hermetically sealing the stage in black. This quite obviously would restrict the flow of actors on and offstage! The need for compromise will always be present and the decisions made about masking will depend on the creative rationale of the designer and director.

When positioning the blacks for masking there will be a number of considerations to take into account; flying space, lighting angles, entrances and exits, scene change movements. The standard method is to start the masking process from downstage with the number one border, with a pair of legs hanging just upstage so that the border masks the bar the legs are hung on. A lighting bar is then positioned directly upstage of the legs and so on up to the cyclorama.

DRAWING PLANS

I have through the course of this chapter referred to the drawing and use of plans and sections to establish sightlines and the position of masking. To effect this a scale has to be used that will produce drawings of an acceptable working size when the full-size venue and set are scaled down on page for the purposes of production and construction drawings. It is important that when drawing out a venue on paper for the first time the extremities of the auditorium can be contained on the piece of paper you selected. Most professional drawings are done on A0/A1 sizes, but A2/A3 may be sufficient for a small venue.

Scales are generally selected in order to bring the set/venue down to a viable working size using a convenient number of units to suit the type of measurement ie: 1:50 (metric), 1:24 (imperial). The ratio written in this way means that 50 units on stage is represented by one unit on paper and vice versa. If the units are metres then '50' metres on stage will be '1' metre on paper; 50 cm will be 1 cm on paper. The same can apply to imperial measurement: with a ratio of 1:24 an inch on the plan would represent two feet on stage. This conversion can be done using conventional rulers and a little arithmetic. There are, however, scale rules, where with a scale of, say, 1:50 the edge of the ruler is marked off in 1 metre units with scaled units of 10 cm between each mark. This can make your life that bit easier, as you don't have to do any calculations.

Always draw in pencil, soft enough for you to rub out when needed. It is a good idea to draw onto tracing paper with the venue plan underneath it, which will give you more flexibility than if you draw directly onto the venue plan.

There are a number of conventions when drawing plans which can be helpful:

- All drawings must be identified through the use of a legend which is positioned in the bottom right-hand corner of every drawn sheet. When the sheet is folded it should be with the legend uppermost. Each legend must contain the following information:

Theatre:
Production: "Title of the Play"
Director:
Designer:
Drwn. by: Date:
Scale: Drwg. no:

2.12 (a) Legend as seen on production drawings

- A setting line is indicated with a long dashed broken line. This is very often an arbitrary line drawn to denote the position from which the scenery will be set.

- A centre line is established precisely at right angles to the setting line; it runs up and downstage, bisecting the setting line and auditorium at its central point. This line is drawn using a chain link from (i.e. dot, dash, dot, dash).

- Sightlines are drawn as shown earlier in this chapter (p. 29).

- If part of the scenery does not touch the stage floor it is drawn with a short dashed line. Door openings are also drawn using a dashed line to show the gap in the architrave and the flat. The same applies to windows.

- A rostrum is drawn as an outline with two diagonal lines across the unit with the height marked (see fig 2:12(b)).

- Steps are marked showing the outline of the tread of the step with a directional arrow. The height of each step is written on it. (The horizontal part of a step is called the tread. The vertical part is called the riser.)

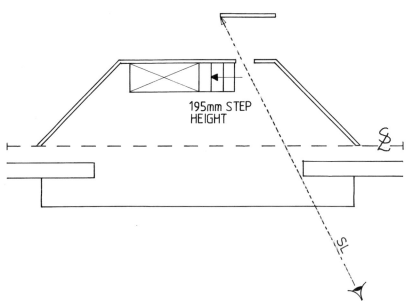

195mm STEP HEIGHT

2.12 (b) Plan drawing showing simple box type with treads, rostra and masking flats showing setting line.

3. Pre-production Planning

MANAGING PEOPLE

People need to know what they are supposed to be doing, obvious but often forgotten.

The stage management team should be able to adjust to any working environment. This means that the roles of each member of the team has to frequently be reviewed. You can help those who work for you by clearly defining what you expect them to be responsible for and the goals in each area of their work.

This can best be done by writing out a brief definition of the task that must be done along with a clear statement of what is required to satisfactorily complete them. This is not to produce a 'That's not my job' culture and it will not. This process does not preclude the creation of joint tasks nor does it dictate that these are the only tasks to be done. It does amongst other things allow prioritisation of tasks. It also gives those working for you (and yourself) an element of freedom while increasing their job satisfaction. This is possible because your team is able to assess if a job is finished and gain satisfaction from this while also being able to get on with the next one. Having people continually coming back to you asking 'What do I do next' may have appeal to your ego for a short time but in the long term it is tedious and rotten management.

When you review the work of others (as you should) look for the positives and when you see good work, tell them. Too often people only get feedback when things are wrong and what is needed is encouragement when things are done well. This will increase the likelihood of it being done so again. However praise should be treated like caviar, if it is spread around like marmalade it soon loses it's appeal and it's subsequent effect.

When you are giving someone credit for a job well done look them in the eye and keep it short, simple and focused on the behaviour of the person. i.e. 'You did a really good job of sorting out Mr Actor and his concerns over using the wind up gramophone'. This focuses on the acknowledgement of behaviour. If this was done with reference to the character of the individual i.e. 'Your people skills never cease to amaze me and that business over the gramophone was no exception' you could be in deep water if the next time you have to pull them up on their interaction with an actor and in reply you get 'Hey the last time you said I was great with people' it will be thought even if it is not said. This aside, whether praising or reprimanding anybody stick to the behaviour of the individual – behaviour can in most cases be relatively easily adjusted. The fundamental characteristics of a person are not so simple.

Along with encouragement of your staff through acknowledgement of the things they do very well, you must also pull them up when things are not. It is best to do this as soon as possible after the event. Don't let things fester, get it out of the way. A sure fire way of generating resentment is at the end of a week you go to a staff member with a string of failings, it will look as if you are keeping a book on their mistakes and ignoring their victories.

Again as with acknowledgement of their successes look them in the eye and keep it short, simple and focused on their behaviour. Looking them in the eye will ensure that you communicate what you feel about it but don't leave it there, you must follow through. The follow through in this situation should be an affirmation of your overall belief in their abilities assuring them that you think they are OK and part of the team. This is most important. Everyone makes mistakes, how else are we to find out what works and what doesn't. Yes, people can be trained but there is often a great many things that require 'doing' in a live situation before they can be truly mastered. Just think of your first driving lesson, what was your problem? You had been watching people doing it for years. Why couldn't you just jump in the car and do it? A last thought in this area is to make sure that you have seen the error yourself, third party hearsay is very dangerous and if your facts are wrong you will not have a leg to stand on.

In summary, if you make people around you feel good about themselves they will produce better results. Make sure your staff know what is required of them and if they don't know how to do something – show them. Look for the positives but if you have to pull someone up, make sure that you finish on a positive. Remember none of us are perfect!

When solving problems with your staff don't solve the problem for them solve it with them. Look for their solutions and help them find the best one. Doing it this way means that next time when they are confronted with a similar problem they may well be able to solve it themselves.

'The Ego Has Landed' I heard one lighting operator say on intercom as the director slipped into the back of the stalls in performance. So what is this thing about creative egos? Ego is why some things that should happen don't, why other things that shouldn't happen do, and why either way they both take longer than they should. Working in the theatre requires the ability to work with people who very often sport large egos. A large ego is not necessarily robust, in fact they are very often the most fragile and inversely the small ego often turns out to be the stronger. The extremely assertive big ego is often the result of a low self image and people like this can often not afford to let things go undone, which can sometimes be an advantage. The one to watch out for is of course your own. Be aware of your strengths and weaknesses and how they may colour your reaction to others. It's difficult to have an insight into others when your own ego is in the way.

PLANNING – THE PLAY, THE VENUE AND THE MONEY

The decision to put on a play may be made by many people or by an individual. The intention will be to get others to come and see the play for without an audience of some kind it would cease to be theatre.

Even at this point it has to be noted that some plays lend themselves to large audiences and others to small; equally, some flourish with lavish staging where others do not. It would be fair to say that every play that was ever written requires certain resources to achieve the writer's intentions. Thankfully, however, directors' perceptions of a writer's intentions are often as variable as the resources available.

The 'resources' can be taken to represent all the elements which together create a performance: people, talent and money, combined with space and ingenuity. The subtle blending of these elements is an art form in itself, as many designers and directors in both the commercial and subsidised theatre have proved.

A production of *Hamlet* without an actor sufficiently talented to perform the lead will fall flat on its face, just as a production of *42nd Street* with too few dancers would fail to have the required impact. But actors are not all that is needed, of course. Carpenters and scene painters must have the flair to recreate a complex design effectively. Lighting and sound designers need both creative verve and the technical competence to execute their concepts in a viable way. The quality of the company and production staff will in part be dependent on the level of finance available for both equipment and manpower. Investment in competent staff can often result in savings in materials and equipment and, most importantly, time and tempers. Remember a play can be lit just as badly with three hundred lanterns as it can with six; technology alone will never provide the whole answer. A large degree of resource management will inevitably be needed and the production/stage manager will almost certainly be involved with this. It is very important that those involved in choosing a play assess its relationship to the proposed venue – not only with regard to getting the right balance of overheads and revenue, but also in terms of establishing the right sort of connection between audience and actors. Shows that require expensive staging on a large scale, from *My Fair Lady* to *Miss Saigon*, will always be given a large theatre that will enable realistic recoupment of the initial investment and a better prospect of profit. (In the case of the subsidized theatre, a greater source of revenue.)

Some amateur and all subsidized professional theatre have, for the most part, fixed financial resource in the form of funding. This, when balanced with projected box office takings gives a budget for the year that allows for the presentation of popular plays and those of more limited interest. Unlike commercial theatre those involved very often cannot go looking for a substitute theatre for they are stuck with the one they have. The audience for their part are also stuck with it, unless theatre companies can transform it for them. This is where ingenuity in the use of space will always overshadow simplistic buying power. I would be the first one to say that money helps and I believe there should be more of it in the arts, but true creative ingenuity is without price.

In many cases in the subsidized theatre, the budget precedes the play as it is part of an overall budget that has to balance both creatively and financially at the end of the year. In the commercial theatre the play will always precede the budget as it is the play and its potential players that will generate the money which leads to its eventual production.

Another cost to consider is copyright. It may be that the play will have to be cleared for copyright with the copyright holder who, in a published work, will be named in the front of the text. In Britain many amateur rights have been bought by a large agency, Samuel French, who administer the copyright. It is rare to get professional copyright clearance for a new play that is in its first year. When applying for a performing licence you must state the proposed dates and the venues, so these have to be agreed at an early stage. When producing reading copies beware that photocopying published text is against the law and could have extreme consequences. Professional stage managers are rarely involved in the clearance of copyright but they are often involved in the sourcing of reading copies. More about copyright is found in Appendix 2, page 121.

CONCEPT AND COST

Once the play is agreed it will require a budget that must reflect both the production costs and the hire of the venue and the detailed business of balancing the director's concept with the cost of realizing his ideas will begin. Sometimes the venue is integral to the concept, and will have formed the starting point for the whole process. Usually the director and designer have a number of meetings to thrash out the basic design format; at an early stage this will be bounced off the production manager who will make technical suggestions and start the budgeting process. From this meeting a number of small meetings will be held, and the concept will develop in tandem with the castings. Depending on the nature of the play a lighting designer, sound designer and wardrobe master/mistress may be consulted early on to advise on cost, concept and technical feasibility. The nature of departmental involvement at this stage will depend on the availability and cost of the relevant staff. In a large company with full-time staff their services are called on as required. In a more commercial situation the various requirements would be put out to quote.

When getting a quotation for a production cost get the best you can. This does not mean the most advantageous price, for that goes without saying, and it is usually the desire to get the best price that causes some people to cut corners in the process. To get a good quote you must provide a good brief which must define: what you want in detail, when you want it, where you want it and the form you want the costs in, i.e. not just one large figure but broken down into it's component parts. Other things to watch out for are: insurance – is it? Who pays? Delivery and collection – cost and when can they do it? Taxes – such as VAT in the United Kingdom and the longevity of the quote – you will need one that will still be valid when you come to do the play.

Asking for quotes is, however, only possible when enough of the concept has been realized to allow for evaluating the actual costs of the proposed scheme. First the production manager will have to develop a basic budget with cost allocations that represent a proportional breakdown of the anticipated expenditure. This can act as a guide in the initial stages. The component parts of this preliminary budget will depend enormously on what is costed as an existing overhead and what as a direct production cost.

The creation of a detailed budget is usually in the hands of the production manager. In the subsidised theatre this will be from an allocation of money usually made earlier in the season before detailed information is available on the production. In the commercial theatre it is more likely grown with the concept of the production and costed in time to allow a calculation of the initial funding required and the box-office returns needed to recoup. Good budgeting and optimism do not go very well together, one must expect the worst as that's usually what you get. To the uninitiated it is useful to know the three fundamentals: cost, quality and speed. Of these elements you can only have two at any one time i.e. quality and speed but not reasonable cost, or speed and reasonable cost but not quality. This is one good reason for forward planning!

The area that must be avoided in any budget is 'guessarama' and wherever possible quotes should be obtained for each requirement in the production. Over and above the cost of the theatre, director, designers and actors there is the cost of staging and staff. These are usually divided into departments such as scenic workshop, wardrobe, sound, lighting, properties, special effects, stage management and show crew. As a rule you must remind yourself that it's people that spend money – carpenters use piles of wood, seamstresses use piles of cloth, electricians need piles of cable and something to go on the end and the list goes on. This can be redressed in part through the use of stock flats, costume and lights if they exist but bear the concept in mind.

For the stage manager there are a few things not to forget. Check:

1. The number of show crew you will need or is allocated at an early stage,

2. Make sure that an allocation of budget for rehearsal props is made,

3. Relative to the budget agree at an early stage what is scenery and what is going to be regarded as props,

4. Make sure that there is an adequate allocation of the budget for consumables/running costs. Examples of these could include:

>   floor cleaning equipment and agents
>   specialist make-up
>   stage management 'blacks' for scene
>   changes
>   spare blades for the swords in sword
>   fights
>   photocopies (not scripts)
>   tape for marking and binding
>   prop food and drink
>   paint for the floor
>   cigarettes and other combustibles
>   blood (more expensive than you think)
>   wig dressing

>   laundry costs
>   SM torches and batteries
>   SM sundries i.e. stationary

This list may not seem like much but this host of little things can mount up to rather a lot of money and if there is no budget you won't have it!

In London's West End all the costs are direct production costs whereas in a subsidized theatre the only direct production costs are often just the set, costumes, lighting and sound – all the other costs are part of the subsidized permanent venue and staff. In a situation such as this a production manager is very often trying to encourage the imaginative use of existing stock flats, furniture and costumes and spread the cost across more than one production.

In most situations, however, the one key element is staffing. A budget will have to be drawn up for the cost of the actors. This is fairly straightforward as the play will in most cases require a specific number of performers. The budget will, however, also have to include travel, subsistence, performance and understudy wages with an allocation for potential overtime if required. For the production manager, staffing requirements are not so clearcut. How many people will it take to do a scene change? How many people will it take to do the set turn round and how long will it take? How many dressers will be needed? How many stage management? How much overtime? At this early budgeting stage there are a lot of discussions and little information to work with – this is where experience steps in! In fact, many of the answers to these questions will be found in the creation of a production schedule. By the time the overall concept has been arrived at, the designer will have produced a scale model and plans of the proposed staging. It is now time for the production manager to convene the first of many full production meetings.

THE PRODUCTION MEETING

Production meetings are a must. They are an opportunity for all the heads of department to liaise with the director and designer. So many production decisions affect more than just one department, and communication is crucial. The nature and colour of set and costumes affect the lighting designer. The position of the lighting equipment can affect scene changes and masking. The positioning of speakers and microphones can affect the set build and costumes. The lateral links are endless and the production meeting is the forum for debate on these subjects. The scale model assists here but a plan and section of the stage will be required when flying bars, lighting positions, sound positions and even prompt corner positions are under discussion.

Each element of the production should be discussed with the production manager taking the chair:

1 Set building
2 Lighting
3 Sound
4 Costume
5 Props
6 Flying
7 Scene changes
8 Schedules
9 Rehearsal notes

When preparing for a meeting make sure that you draft an agenda that displays clear goals rather than the obligatory list of departments that needs discussion. This agenda can and should be compiled with the help of the HODs. This agenda can then be circulated at the meeting and used as the check list for all those present. For this reason it is worth spending a little time working out the best order for the topics to be discussed.

When starting the meeting remind everyone how long has been allocated for the meeting and check that no one has any time constraints. It must be said that they should all have kept this time free in their diary as production meetings are pivotal in the production process. Working through the agenda the chairman's questions should be focused and not just the general 'Is everything OK with you in wardrobe Jenny?' It is *not* always the case but I would suggest that for this sort of review the stage management is divided into two – a report from the stage manager covering subjects such as scene changes and production schedules plus a report from the DSM on progress in rehearsal and a round up of issues arising from the rehearsal notes.

During the meeting it is important to keep notes of the decisions made and the agreed action points. At the end of the meeting it can be useful to round up the notes into a small summary for general agreement. The notes can then be typed up and distributed among the attendees.

As these meetings progress more information will be brought to the meeting in the form of:

1 Provisional list of lighting cues and states, see fig. 3:1.
2 Provisional list of sound cues and effects, see fig. 3:2.
3 Provisional props lists, see fig. 3:3.
4 Provisional costume plot and changes
5 Flying plots
6 Running plots
7 Construction drawings
8 Rehearsal notes.

Provisional lists and plots will be tabled and amended further as information from rehearsals is made available and the technical specifications are developed. This allows the requirements of the production to be both addressed and advanced, and will in turn lead on to more detailed staffing allocations and further budget implications. In production meetings the word budget will not be far from the lips of those present. This meeting will also be where a production schedule is devised that covers the length of time which will be spent on stage from fit-up to first nights. Any schedule must be commensurate with the time and money available.

SCHEDULING

The importance of good scheduling at this stage for any production cannot be over-emphasized. The use of wardrobe, stage workshop and rehearsal space and actors must be well planned out beforehand. With a very simple modern production involving six actors and a standing set the process can be very straightforward but if there is to be a chorus of twenty with a dozen principals, fifteen sets and an orchestra, the forward planning is the key to the success of the whole production. This scheduling process will involve all the heads of department but chiefly the production manager, the stage manager and the director.

In its rough form the rehearsal schedule is presented to the cast at the first reading when they are informed of the times and siting of rehearsals for the coming weeks. A schedule may include wig fittings, costume fittings, music rehearsals, dance rehearsals, fight rehearsals, special rehearsals (for things

THE BUS AND TRUCK THEATRE COMPANY

'JOURNEY'S END'

PROVISIONAL LIGHTING PLOT

PAGE	EFFECT
	House lights Tab warmers On stage preset
1	* Fading light of an evening in March * Two lit candles on-stage * Bursts of light seen in sky periodically throughout scene - vari lights * Moonlight in walkway outside dug-out
20	Hibbert lights and exits with candle
25	Osborne blows out candle by Stanhope's bed
26	Final vari light seen in sky with follow on fade to preset with tabs.
	House lights Tab warmers On stage preset
27	Early morning before sunrise Two candles still lit in dug-out
29	Sunrise over 3 minutes
	Square of sunlight to be seen coming through enhance of dug-out.
39	Fade to preset with tabs.
	Bright afternoon sunlight Two candles lit in dug-out Square of light through entrance is no longer visible.

3.1 Provisional lighting plot

such as a meal in *Saturday, Sunday, Monday* or *You Never Can Tell*) or a special effect over and above the normal rehearsals. The director may also wish to indicate when the initial blocking will be complete and when they expect the books to go down, i.e.: the actors are no longer encumbered with scripts. If it is extremely complicated, each member of the company may be given a schedule of rehearsal but at the very least a copy of the basic structure along with maps showing rehearsal rooms should be posted on the call boards along with the dates of the:

technical rehearsal;
the first and second dress rehearsal;
first preview;
press night and first night.

The schedule should naturally be accompanied by a cast list showing the parts to be played, the principals and their understudies. This, like all pieces of production paperwork should have the name of the production and the date it was posted. The initial discussions on scheduling will start with a series of deadlines created by the director, which at its most basic can be 'We open on July 7th!'. From here evolves the plan to which everyone will work. A typical outline is given below:

• Initial designs
• Auditions
• Final designs
• Casting
• Casting complete
• Working drawings complete
• Set building starts
• First reading
• Rehearsals start
• All substitute props in rehearsal

'JOURNEY'S END'

PROVISIONAL SOUND PLOT

PAGE	EFFECT
	House music
	Curtain up music
1	Rumble of guns
2	Machine gun effect
9	Rumble of guns
10	Rumble of guns continues
11	Rumble of guns dies away
12	Rumble of guns
17	Sound of grenades
18	Two shells heard whining overhead
24	Machine gun fire
26	Low rumble of guns
26	Scene change music
Act II Sc. 1	
27	Gun fire carried by wind
32	Two bangs followed by fading whistl
39	Scene change music
53	Interval music

3.2 Provisional sound plot

- First run through in rehearsal
- Prop parade
- Set build complete
- Final external rehearsal
- Get-in
- Fit up
- Lighting focus
- Lighting session
- Dress parade
- Technical rehearsal
- First dress rehearsal
- Second dress rehearsal
- Final dress rehearsal
- First preview
- Press night
- First night
- Last night

From these deadlines will develop the details of rehearsal, particularly the following considerations:

1 The size and numbers of rehearsal and auditorium rooms required and the dates when they will be needed.

2 The opportunities for wardrobe fittings and specialist rehearsals.

3 Over what time period hired items

Auditions Checklist

- Jug of water and cups at the side of the stage.

- Mark the stage or floor to indicate where the lighting has the best effect and explain this to the auditionees.

- Provide a minimum of two chairs, one table and an ashtray.

- In order to reduce noise, distraction and discomfort, make sure there are no actors waiting in the wings.

- Put 'Quiet please' notices round the theatre or rooms hired.

- Wear clean smart clothes but do not wear anything that might detract from the impact of the auditionee.

- Establish with the auditionees what props they need so that these are set for them when they start.

- When announcing, walk onto the stage, call the name of the actor, wait for him/her to pass you and then make your exit.

- Always be polite and helpful but do not infer anything other than professional interest.

- Always obtain the actor's name and address plus the name and address of the agent.

such as weapons, furniture and costumes will be needed – all of which may be different depending on rehearsal requirements.

4 The need to have specialist props in rehearsal.

5 The time and place of the first full mark-out and subsequent additional mark-outs (it is unlikely that a mark-out will be needed for a music rehearsal).

All of these will have an effect on the budgeting of the production. So will the planning of the 'production week' – the period of technical and dress rehearsals at the venue itself (which need not be a week in length of course).

The scheduling and organization of the production week will vary according to the availability of the production space – you may have a show in the evening while you are rehearsing in the day, God forbid – and the availability of staff or specialist kit. The approach should be flexible but with a specific result in mind.

AUDITIONS

The need for auditions is common, if not inevitable. When organizing a set of auditions it is advisable to find a space that is as central as possible and convenient for public transport. If a theatre stage is not available then choose rooms large enough to allow some distance between the director and the auditionees. It helps if the auditionee is well lit but not dazzled by stage lights or sunlight. Provide the auditionees with a table and chair and an ashtray. Names and addresses of agents and auditionees alike should be collected. Each actor should be announced prior to auditioning and you should always check pronunciation for the benefit of the director.

When calling actors to the audition leave approximately ten minutes between each person and ensure that they wait in another room out of earshot. At all times the stage management should be seen to be polite and professional, as this will almost certainly help to put people at ease. I have never heard a director say 'Don't call us, we'll call you' and it would certainly be more than a stage manager's life is worth to say so.

FURTHER PRODUCTION PLANNING

At the same time as the director is selecting the company of actors for the production, the stage manager should be outlining detailed staffing needs and the responsibilities that will be given to those members of staff.

The director will now be drawing together the conceptual threads of the production. The stage-production manager will at this point be leading a split life. He/she will be researching the detail of the production with the designer but will also be continually assessing the cost implications of the director's and designer's ideas. This is a function that also falls to a production manager should there be one.

As the design process develops the stage manager will be responsible for the duplication and distribution of initial lists, plots and drawings to the heads of department. One of the stage manager's principal functions is to create a provisional prop list, costume plot, lighting plot and sound plot, which involves a religious rereading of the text and continual badgering of the departments involved.

Later on a stage manager's life revolves round the company but at this stage when the company has not yet been drawn together his/her energies must be devoted towards the organization of props. The selection of props will be an ongoing process throughout the rehearsal period.

Whether buying, borrowing, making or hiring a prop, the fundamentals come first – what are you looking for? Your research starts with the play, the reading and rereading of the text while compiling a list of all the items found there. The props required may, at first reading be far from obvious: a handkerchief for the crying heroine, a tablecloth for the dinner table or sugar tongs for the *lump* sugar that is such a memorable part of Gwendolen and Cecily's tea together in *The Importance of Being Earnest* – each lump being administered with rapier-like precision.

The provisional prop list should be drawn up stating the following:

1 date of compilation,
2 the play,
3 what it is – 'provisional prop list',
4 who compiled it – Donald Duck, ASM,
5 number of acts,
6 number of scenes,
7 the relevant page numbers in the script being used,
8 notes on each prop,

THE BUS AND TRUCK THEATRE COMPANY

JOURNEY'S END

PROVISIONAL PROPERTY PLOT

Furniture:

2 x Beds
2 x Benches
3 x Boxes (stools)
1 x Table

Dressing:	Sacks	
	Ammunition cases	
	Gas masks	
	Cuttings from magazines	
	Water bottles	
	Ammunition belts	
P.1	2 x candles in bottles - practical	On table
	Boot and sock	p.p. Hardy
	Gas mask	p.p. Hardy
P.2	Helmet	p.p. Osborne
	Pack	p.p. Osborne
	Bottle of whisky & mug	On table
	Pipe	p.p. Osborne
	Assorted papers	On table
P.3	Map	On table
	Cigarettes and matches	p.p. Hardy
	Ashtray	On table
P.4	Tattered equipment list	Under table
P.5	Picture (Paris)	On wall
	Pack (Hardy)	On nail
	Spectacles (Hardy)	In pack
P.6	Tattered log book	On bench
	Rag	On bed
	Tin hat (Hardy)	On nail
	Stick (Hardy)	On bed
	Gas mask	On bed
	Map case	On bed
	Binoculars	On bed
	Compass case	On bed
P.7	2 x newspapers	Set SL wing
P.8	Tin hat	p.p. Raleigh
	Pack	p.p. Raleigh
	Water bottle - practical	On nail
	Tin of cigarettes	On bench

3.3 Provisional property plot

9 if a personal prop, the character to whom it belongs.

The 'notes' section of this list has to be the most important of all. For example, if a candle is listed the note should ask 'is it lit, and if so for how long? Is someone on stage with it all the time?' The answer to this question will determine whether or not the candle used will be real or electric. When the inevitable hanky appears the note may ask 'pocket? colour?' A situation onstage must be created in all its aspects – so we must ask what is the colour, size and material of this hanky, and where it is kept: trouser pocket, dress pocket, top pocket, sleeve? These sort of questions and their answers will develop from the direction and design of the play itself.

A prop list such as this enables early problem analysis to begin. The use of a real flame on stage can be a problem if the requirement is not taken in hand at an early stage. A door that has to be broken down is only a problem if the workshop have already built it.

This initial text research should therefore establish the existence of a prop and its possible use within the play.

Research is also needed to establish the period, style and use of a prop. Take, for example, a samovar; first you need to find out what it looks like and then how it should be used. This could require visits to museums, reference libraries and perhaps art galleries as examples of paintings or photographs of the period can very often be helpful in establishing the mood and overall look of a period. If possible such research is best done in conjunction with the designer, who well may wish to direct the findings towards an overall concept.

It is now time to sit down with the director, designer and production manager to discuss your findings, providing all three with a copy of your props list and details of your research. At this meeting it should be possible to decide what can be added to and deleted from your list, and which items can be immediately actioned. Potential problem areas can also be discussed. You will at this stage be able to identify the need for prop dressing. In Joe Orton's *Loot* a glass eye is supposed to roll from the police inspector's hand, under the bed. This could be a problem as research will show that glass eyes are not round and therefore do not roll! Orton may have known this at the time of writing but again he may not. Either way, there is a need for a rolling eye which in the context of the whole play is not out of place. What about the need for a laughing sailor dummy (life size) required in *Sleuth*? Why not stuff an ASM ask the cast!

You must remind yourself at this stage that what you now have is not the definitive prop list for it will inevitably change through the rehearsal process. Fix a time when all rehearsal props will be ready (a representation of *all* props should, nevertheless, be available in rehearsal). Agree the date of a prop parade at which all the finished props will be signed off with the director. It is also advisable to divide the props list into categories such as:

Practical: props that will be used by actors.

Specialized props and effects: lights, mechanical props, weapons etc.

Set dressing: additional props that are not used during the action of the play but are arranged to enhance the staging.

Personal props: properties carried on the actor's person.

Many of the areas covered on the provisional prop list will be linked with the work of other departments: set building, costume, lighting and sound. To ensure that the lines of communication are kept open it is important that the stage manager copies the relevant information for each department so that it can be discussed at a production meeting. Ideally this meeting will be before the first reading, but props research will, by necessity, be an ongoing process.

BUYING AND HIRING PROPS

When buying and hiring props you must start out knowing exactly what you want and how much money you have to finance the acquisition. There is usually precious little point in going to look at a prop that is out of your price range or totally the wrong thing. When buying an item the first contact is usually a phone call, and this brings us to the first fence at which so many fall. Are you prepared to make the call? Do you have a piece of clean paper in front of you with the day's date, the name of the show and your name on it. If you don't then you are not ready. The 'show, name, date' principle, if held to, will serve you well. How many times have I heard ASM's scrabbling around in the stage management office, looking for a phone number or measurement that has gone walkabout – only to find that it was written on a faceless piece of paper giving no clue as to the owner but for the scrawl of a manic spider.

So provide yourself with a clean labelled piece of paper at the start of every phone call. It will also help to have before you some of the more specific requirements you have with regard to the items you are hiring – availability, period, look, colour, size, weight (you may need to know if they are a one or two man lift for the scene change) and, of course, cost. When establishing the cost you should also establish the method of payment, finding out if the supplier will accept an order, a company cheque, or whether it has to be cash on collection. For your part, you will need either a quotation showing the required method of payment or a proforma invoice to extract a cheque from the management. In most instances you will be required to produce a company order for any large purchase whether the supplier needs it or not and this will have to be signed by an authorized signatory. With regular suppliers it is very often sufficient just to quote an order number which is followed by a written order.

Having established all this information you will then have to have a contact name, a complete address, details of opening hours and what loading or parking is available if required. It would be foolish not to view the goods that you are hiring or buying and a visit should be organized; it is usually best to do this together with the designer. If you are selecting furniture the hire company will require a couple of days to pull out the relevant pieces for your selection. If you just arrive on their doorstep you will have to wait even longer and succeed in getting their backs up.

In many situations it falls to the stage manager to borrow items for use in productions. This very often happens by necessity due to the lack of funds for buying or hiring the objects needed. In this case a bit of judicious borrowing can also allow part of the prop budget to be reallocated to other areas. This should not, however, be taken for granted when drawing up a production budget, as there are many occasions when borrowing is not viable or practical. When touring a show the logisitics of returning a prop become overly complex; with a projected long run the wear and tear on a borrowed item becomes unacceptable.

The business of borrowing, for business

it is, must be approached as a selling exercise. What are you selling? The theatre and the show. It is not enough to say how wonderful the show will be as that is going to do little for the people you hope will lend you the props – you have to convey the idea that there are benefits in it for them too. So, first set up how good the show is going to be, and then follow through with the prospect of free tickets that you are sure that you could sort out with the general manager. You are immediately suggesting to the person that he is being brought into the theatre family – you are, in fact, selling a special relationship with the theatre which helps to ease the proceedings along. If, in the course of conversation you find that they have an interest in a particular aspect of the theatre (which more than likely will not have anything to do with the show in hand) you could develop that. This could take the form of trips round the theatre for their children, tickets to the Sooty Show in two months time, a trip to the opera which visits once a year – but don't promise things you can't deliver. Often I have returned to do battle with the general manager of the theatre in an attempt to obtain complimentary tickets for prospective prop lenders. Getting comps can often be like pulling teeth but in the end if the saving is great enough to include your time in finding another source, then few managers can resist the opportunity to save money.

When going out propping you are an ambassador of the theatre as a whole and your theatre in particular. You have to look and act responsibly, and although this might be a strain, it is a necessity! It is imperative that you know all the details of what you want because whether you are talking to a large chain store or an antique shop they will want it proven that you know what you are talking about. If you are able to walk into an antique shop and refer to 'the Georgian tripod table in the window' rather than 'that one over there' it will be to your benefit. Showing interest in what people do will help to put them at ease and give them the incentive to take an interest in what you are doing and what you want. When approaching a company try and get as close to the top as you can – helpful Harrys in the lower echelons may be full of promises but often cannot produce the goods as they usually make a rotten job of putting your case to the higher management. In your initial approach don't give your potential lender the opportunity to say no before you have had a chance to prove what a worthy cause your theatre is and suggested how good they will feel when they have assisted you with your problem.

Programme credits to those that lend can be sold to some as a further 'benefit' but in my experience people tend to view credits as their right. A small note here to say that a correct programme credit is a boon, a forgotten credit is bad but an incorrect credit is a disaster. Always check that you have written down exactly what must appear in the programme. The best way of doing this is to add the programme credit details to the borrowing receipt and get the lender to sign it. The programme proof is then checked against the receipt.

What is a borrowing receipt? It is an essential part of the system which ensures that the props are returned in good order at the right time to the right person. A receipt book will be given to each ASM who goes out propping; it takes the form of a duplicate book in which the following information is recorded:

1 date,
2 name and address of lender and phone number,
3 items lent – description, including defects and value,

DATE	NAME + ADDRESS	ITEMS	VALUE	DATE BORROWED	TO BE RET'D	BORROWED BY	PROGRAMME CREDIT
1ST AUG.	CRAGSIDE HOUSE ROTHBURY	EDWARDIAN INLAID TABLE (CHIPPED LEG)	£500	25TH JULY	25TH AUG	J.B.	CRAGSIDE HOUSE
1ST AUG.	CRAGSIDE HOUSE ROTHBURY	GRANDFATHER CLOCK (NOT TICKING)	£275	25TH JULY	25TH AUG	J.B.	CRAGSIDE HOUSE
3RD AUG.	MORNINGSIDE MANOR	STANDING LAMP (BRASS)	£100	30TH JULY	30TH AUG	D.B.	MORNINGSIDE MANOR

3.4 Borrowing book

4 date to be returned,
5 signature of lender, *also in printed form,*
6 signature of borrower,
7 credit to be given in programme.

The lender should be given the top copy and the carbon stays in the duplicate book. The book itself should have on its cover the stamp of the theatre and the ASM's name which can act as identification. When the items are returned the top copy of the receipt must be retrieved. An explanation of this process can be used in the early stages to reassure the lender when you first introduce yourself and explain exactly who you are.

The contents of the receipt books will then be transferred into a main 'borrowing book' which acts as the information base for all items hired, borrowed or stolen for the production. Its layout would be as shown in the fig. 3:4 .

You will note the inclusion of the overall value of items detailed in the main book. It is important you ensure that the theatre has adequate insurance to cover the items borrowed. There does, however, come a point at which it is inadvisable to borrow a property if the risk of damage is too high.

Borrowing is not easy and it is not always the most cost effective way of doing things but it still has its place in many avenues of theatre. Once you have proved to an individual or a company that it is both beneficial and fun to lend to the theatre, you can save a great deal of money and obtain a higher grade of prop. In smaller towns it can add to the community support for the local theatre by getting people involved – you can enhance this feeling by having a Christmas party for all those who have supported the theatre over the year or the season.

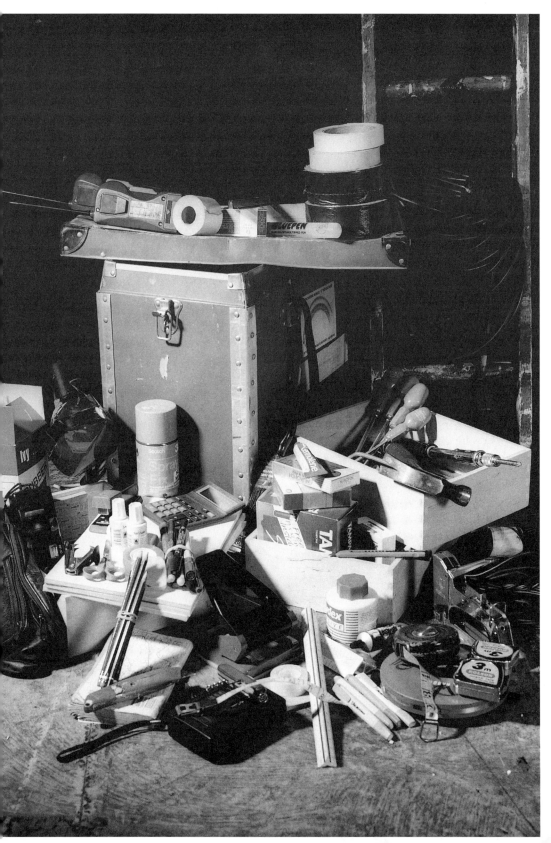

4. *Rehearsal Planning*

THE REHEARSAL SCHEDULE

A well organized rehearsal schedule is the key to dealing effectively with the stage management workload.

A rehearsal schedule will need to be constructed which anticipates the practical needs of the cast and director in rehearsal. For a production with a standing set and six characters this will not be a particularly trying task but for a musical the schedule would have to include the teaching and rehearsal of solo numbers, the teaching and rehearsal of dance numbers and the rehearsal of acting scenes. Such rehearsals have difference space requirements and all actors will have to go to wardrobe fittings, so with this sort of production the rehearsal scheduling has to be done well in advance. It is also necessary nowadays to take into account the permitted working hours of an acting company both in performance and rehearsal. There are limits laid down by Equity, the actor's union, and the technically affiliated unions detailing a fixed number of hours that can be worked by a performer without overtime. If overtime is worked you must be sure that there is a budgetary allocation for it and that any such overtime is monitored. Overtime payment is one of the reasons why it is essential that rehearsal time is very carefully structured.

To assist with the construction of a rehearsal schedule, a chart can be drawn up to show who is present in which scene, called the 'availability chart' (see fig. 4:1 opposite). Down the left-hand column it shows the names of the actor and the character; in the top horizontal spaces the scenes of the play are listed. Quite simply, if an actor is in a scene a cross is indicated on the chart. A simple but effective device to aid the organization of rehearsals.

This chart will also assist the wardrobe department to quick changes and help with the general costume organization.

THE REHEARSAL SPACE

The choice of rehearsal rooms can be crucial to the whole production process for if the space is in any way inadequate it will be reflected in the mood of those working there. It is not unknown for this mood to end up on the stage of the theatre having been transferred from the rehearsal room. A good way of finding a suitable space can be through advertising in the local press; if this does not bear fruit then a visit to the local church institutions may well produce a result.

The size of the actual rehearsal space must match the staging needs of the play. In this calculation you must remember to leave a good 3 metres (10 ft) in front of the marked-out stage for the director's and stage manager's desks. It can also be extremely useful to have a small space to each side which serves as a seating area for those actors involved in the scene that is being rehearsed but who have not yet

BUS & TRUCK Co 'The Sea'	SCENE 1	SCENE 2	SCENE 3	SCENE 4	SCENE 5	SCENE 6	SCENE 7	SCENE 8
Willy Carson – Adam Hall	X	X	X	X		X	X	X
Evans – Matthew Henshaw	X	X	X				X	X
Hatch – Michael Johnson	X	X			X	X	X	X
Hollarcut – Richard Tierney	X				X	X	X	X
Vicar – Thomas Allan				X		X	X	X
Carter – Matt Bond		X	X		X	X		
Thompson – Ben James		X	X					
Louise Fafi – Beverley Winn		X	X			X		
Rose Jones – Jenny Mylove				X	X		X	X
Jessica Tilehouse – Lynne Martindale		X		X	X			
Mafanwy Price – Verna Smith				X			X	X
Jilly – Elaine Michaels				X			X	X
Rachel – Nicola Phillips				X			X	X
Davis – Brittany Bainbridge				X			X	X

4.1 *Availability chart*

entered. Most important, people must be able to come to and fro from rehearsal without disrupting the action in progress. Ideally a separate room should be provided that can act as a green room, with a facility for refreshments. If there is a kitchen then this room should be adjacent to it so as to prevent the inevitable stream of actors through the rehearsal space en route to coffee.

The acoustics of the space should not be so lively as to cause interference to normal conversation. It is also wise to ensure that there are no external noises that will cause disruption to the rehearsal process. Always ensure that there are adequate lavatory facilities for the number of men and women involved in the rehearsal.

Other practical considerations to be taken into account, more for the benefit of the stage management, are access and storage. Size of doorways can be crucial

when bringing in pieces of scenery or furniture. There may also be time or access restrictions that have to be thought of. Storage space can be extremely useful for rehearsal props and furniture and can often save time and frustration. It's also worth finding out who else is using the space other than yourselves – will the bible class take pleasure in picking your trace marks off the floor, necessitating a completely new mark-out.

It is important to establish a sound contract when renting space. You must ensure that you determine the complete nature of your responsibilities and the responsibilities of the organization you are renting from. In relation to this, it is important to ascertain whether there is enough heat and light and who is responsible for billing. Other matters that need to be researched and checked are the availability of additional power and the form it takes; the cost and availability of local car parking, local shopping and opening items. During rehearsal the demands made of these facilities will undoubtedly be greater than is usual. As with any other venue, you will also need to have the full postal address and telephone number with the contact's name and home number.

When the cast list is complete and the date for the first reading is set, it is time to mail out the first communication from the stage management to the cast. This will contain a copy of the script (unless the director requests otherwise) and a call sheet for the first reading which also contains the address and telephone number of the rehearsal room with a map and indication of public transport and parking facilities. A cast list should also be included with a brief schedule of the pre-production process. With this package winging its way to the newly selected company there is just time to sort out a few other outstanding matters.

There are a few occasions when special licences are required. These very often take some time to process through the authorities and it is important that they are actioned as soon as the need for them is established. Children, firearms, exotic animals and live fire effects all require either special licences or local authority clearance. I can see a number of ways in which you could link these, but the one common factor has to be that they are all dangerous on stage!

Sometimes a stage manager will be required to arrange for specialist skills to be taught in rehearsal. These can include fight direction, choreography, vocal coaching and musical direction. If any or indeed all of these things are to happen then facilities will have to be made available in the rehearsal space.

By this time the director and the designer will have completed their staging concept and a scale model of the stage and the set will have been made, which will be presented along with costume drawings at the first reading.

With all this done it is only left to the stage manager to browse through a copy of *Spotlight* (or in the US *Players Guide*) to ensure that he can put a name to a face when he meets the company for the first time in the first reading.

Rehearsal Space Checklist

- Ensure the space is large enough for your needs

- Establish contractual obligations regarding heat and light

- Ensure there are sufficient additional facilities – green room, lavatories, kitchen

- Establish access, time and door sizes plus available storage

- Investigate local parking, shopping and transport facilities

- Full postal address, telephone number of rehearsal rooms and the contact's home telephone number

Rehearsal Checklist

- Check names and addresses are held for all the cast and company

- Maintain time sheets for all the cast and stage management

- Liaise with Equity Deputy

- Organise coffee money, if Management do not pay

- Supply of all rehearsal props

- Give running times to the Management and Front of House

- Weekend addresses of company must be left

- Check all props in and out of rehearsal

- Post and note all calls and schedules

- Pass on all rehearsal notes to relevant departments

- Keep the prompt script up to date

- Check mark-out remains accurate throughout rehearsal

- Keep details of all costume and wig fittings

- Organise head of departments from sound, lighting and costume to visit rehearsals

5. *The Rehearsal Process*

THE FIRST READING

The first day of rehearsal is preceded by a first reading which has to be viewed as one of the key stages in the growth of the production. The purpose of the first reading is for all of the acting company to sit down and read the text without being encumbered with moves, props and scenery. This first reading provides a platform for the director to present his principal concepts to the people who are about to embark on a creative journey with him. At the beginning of a first reading it has been known for directors to read passages of poetry, display paintings and mime events in their own life in an attempt to convey their deepest feelings about the play.

The first reading is an excellent opportunity to present the working disciplines round which you will run the activities of the company through rehearsal and performance. This does not mean that you present them as an edict from the mount but it also does not mean that they are mumbled in a corner. As mentioned earlier people like to know where they stand and in the long run they will be glad to have the key information upfront. For instance; ask for contact telephone numbers for people at weekends in case schedules change; liaise with wardrobe to ensure costume calls for actors don't clash with rehearsals.

Practically, the space for this event should be large enough to accommodate not just those who are performing but all those involved in putting on the play: as a minimum, the sound, lighting, set and costume designers and the wardrobe mistress/master should be present, but the event should be attended by every possible person who may be involved, down to those who make tea in the workshop.

The stage management should therefore make allowance in the seating numbers for all those who may be attending. The seating format should ideally be a horseshoe with a tall table at the end on which the set model can be positioned, with the director and the designer to left and right. Coffee should be served as the meeting begins and the stage manager, having grown familiar with the faces of the cast through careful study of *Spotlight*, is in an ideal position to form introductions on a social level, prior to the start of the reading. There will come an opportunity later when the stage manager should introduce all those present by going round the horseshoe and saying which character each actor will be playing, and describing the technicians' functions. As the actors arrive, stage management should confirm with the members of the company their home address, their current address (if different) and their agent's name and telephone number. A contact sheet can then be typed up by the stage management and issued to the director and retained by the stage management for whom it will be an extremely vital piece of paperwork.

When all are seated, and with the

agreement of the director, the stage manager should formally introduce those present and hand over to the director. The director will, as I described, wish to make some sort of conceptual statement that will help everyone to understand the approach he is going to take. Most directors will then suggest that 'the best thing we can do now is to read the play'. (The stage management must ensure that there are sufficient reading copies available for everybody present.)

As the reading begins the stage manager will start his stopwatch so as to take an initial timing on the reading of the play. This timing will in the long run prove to be totally inaccurate (too short) due to the lack of action, but it does help to get an overall understanding of the timing of the piece.

When the reading is complete the director will then reintroduce the designer and together they will unveil the model box and talk the company through the contents of the design. This could take place before the reading and the structure of the reading should be discussed with the director. It is extremely important that the company understand the physical nature of the design and that is indeed one of the purposes of producing the model box at the first reading. The costume designs will then be shown to the cast and there may be a brief discussion on the nature of the characters and the nature of the costumes. Given that this is only the first reading it is rare for any definitive decisions to come from this discussion.

When the discussion is over the stage manager will then have an opportunity to present the rehearsal schedule to the company. It is best to have the schedule typed up and distributed at this point to allow any questions that may need answering to come to the surface. At the same time the stage manager can explain how to get to the rehearsal rooms and where the call boards for the production will be situated, i.e.: stage call board, green room call board, rehearsal call board and theatre switchboard. If the wardrobe have requested that the cast report at an early stage to wardrobe, the stage manager should outline the scheduling of these visits and also where the wardrobe is to be found.

The proceedings will then be adjourned, usually until the following day when the real process of rehearsal will begin.

INTO REHEARSAL

Rehearsals are the seed beds in which the production is nurtured by the director. It must therefore be a protected environment in which the production can grow with minimal disruption from outside forces. In many cases the cast have not met before and the director is new, as is the environment. Everyone in the company must work to establish a real bond of trust based on the belief that all those involved will deliver what is required to create a truly effective production.

The director has a vision of the play, which will be expressed through both the interpretation of the text and the design concepts – yet he also needs understanding of the processes of staging a performance. This will involve dealing with actors' insecurities, misunderstandings, egos and the mechanics of production. In short, the director will need all the help he can get.

The actor, on the other hand, will have to cope with a director who 'does not understand', keeps putting him or her down, a text that is almost impossible to learn, digs that are not suitable and 'blocking that would be better suited to a Sandhurst parade ground, Darling'. It is not easy to come to terms with the failings of others when you are still trying to come to terms with your own ability to fulfil your role. The actors will also need both practical and personal help to get through the assault course called the rehearsal period.

The cast, stage management, director and designer are a team who, if motivated with a good concept and supported by teamwork, can move mountains. The stage management can ensure that the right environment is provided for the rehearsal process by anticipating problems and dealing with the practical issues of production efficiently and sensitively while maintaining a sense of humour.

During this period there a number of issues that the stage manager must deal with outside rehearsal. The publicity department will require staffing and credits information for the compilation of the programme. These details will then need to be checked when the programme proof is produced prior to printing. Liaison with the FOH management is important even at this early stage. They will need approximate timings to assess staffing levels and general information about the production for the box office. As a stage manager you will have to work closely with the FOH manager and agree the procedure for opening the house to let the audience in, giving clearance for the curtain up and emergency procedures. Do remember that you are both in a position to help each other.

When rehearsals start, a number of directors like to introduce 'trust' games, which always get a mixed reception. They have their worth, for in practice the production will grow from the trust between all parties concerned, so it can only benefit the stage management to join in. Trust games can be fun and are often very enlightening, both with regard to yourself and others.

The first stage in the rehearsal will be the blocking, where the director sets the basic moves to be made by the actors while spouting their lines. This is not usually regarded as a major interpretive feature but it will have been structured by the director from a lot of textual analysis. The process of blocking allows everyone to write their moves into their text. There is no fixed method of directing blocking, for a number of directors will allow actors to find their own positions in the initial stages. As the rehearsals progress these first moves will develop into a cohesive whole. Whatever the approach, blocking will require an accurate replica of the stage to be created in the rehearsal room. This usually takes the form of a two dimensional representation on the floor of the rehearsal room called 'the mark-out'. It can also be useful to have the model available at this point to assist the imaginations of all concerned.

THE MARK-OUT

A mark-out is an easily read, full-size replica of the ground plan of the stage, with scenic walls, steps, doors, windows and masking. It gives the actor and the director a clear understanding of the acting area available, and the entrances and exits. The exits must be clearly marked to the correct scale. To create this full-size layout you must have an up-to-date ground plan at a scale of 1:50 metric or 1:24 imperial, and a scale rule that will give you accurate measurements from the ground plan. Nowadays, it is possible to acquire scale rules that convert from metric to imperial and vice versa and this will help those who are mentally tied to one scale or another. There is no reason, however, for you not to be conversant with both.

When marking out it is important to

leave space at the front for the director to view the rehearsal and to provide a position for the DSM to sit at a table and make notes in the prompt script. If possible, the door to the rehearsal room should be in a position which will cause minimal distraction and yet be accessible, i.e. behind the director. If the room has any major distractions, such as mirrors, they should be covered. If the area is restricted and it is the only place you have to rehearse, discuss the position of the stage in the rehearsal room with the director, for there may be areas that are deemed more important than others for that particular rehearsal. Where possible mark what the elements are on the floor (such as steps with a directional arrow). The use of spare chairs or wooden poles to mark each side of entrances and along walls can help prevent the actor from walking through walls in rehearsal. Coloured tape used to denote different elements of the set or different scenes can help the actor. However, all of the rehearsal will be under the watchful eye of the stage manager who should pick up on any misinterpretation of the mark-out and explain the error to those concerned. Unless you are rehearsing for *Blithe Spirit*, walking through walls, even in rehearsal, is not recommended!

When rehearsing a show that involves a front cloth (see glossary) it can be useful to have two posts with a rope between the length of the setting line. This can be drawn across the marked out stage to prevent the actors from getting overly excited about the amount of space available for the scene. Where possible, rostra should be provided to denote raised levels on the stage. If this is not possible then two or three-tread sets of steps should be provided to give a better sense of the interaction between actors as they exit and enter.

The materials for marking out are as follows:

Chalk
Snap line
Two long measuring tapes,
    i.e. 100 ft (30.5 metres)
Ground plan
Scale rule
Pencil
Sticky tape
Short measuring tape,
    i.e. 10 ft (3.5 metres)
Cutting board for tape

NB The tape used should ideally be ½ inch webbed cloth tape. This does not stretch like PVC tape and it tears more easily than PVC. PVC does have the habit of creeping along the floor when it has been laid out, leaving a nasty mess when it is pulled up – **beware of damaging floor surfaces.**

The mark-out should take place before the cast arrive and at least two hours should be allowed for the first mark-out of a simple set to give time to decide on the orientation of the layout within the room. It can save a lot of time if you have written the set measurements onto the ground plan before arriving at the rehearsal venue.

To orientate the set within the space, it is useful to start with a longitudinal reference, i.e. the centre line, and a latitudinal reference, i.e. the setting line (see fig. 5:1). The centre line is the line drawn down the centre of a drawing in long and short dashes marked [⌀]. The setting line is usually positioned arbitrarily between the upstage line of the proscenium arch and the start of the flattage, sometimes along the tab line, and marked [⌀].

These two lines can assist enormously in the positioning of the set and can be laid down using a snap line. The powdered chalk lines left on the floor from a snap line will quickly fade. As the lines themselves will be of no direct use during the

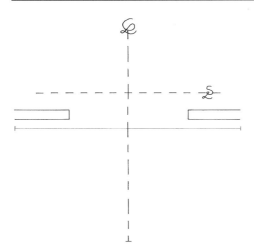

5.1 Setting line and centre line

rehearsal it does not matter that they will fade. It can, however, be useful to indicate in some way the stage curtain and safety curtain lines, so that these can be taken into account when positioning furniture.

In the mark-out of a studio set it can also be useful to create a setting line so, once again, the set can be orientated. If the setting line is given a finite length in a theatre with a proscenium arch (the width of the proscenium, for example) these two points can provide the reference from which the rest of the set may be marked

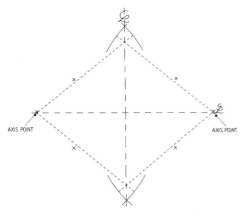

5.2 Finding the centre line

out. Working from these points using long tape measures bisecting arches can be drawn with chalk to indicate the key features of the set. All that has to be done after that is to join the dots.

This method can be used to mark-out the centre line by bisecting arches of the same length both above and below the setting line. When the points created above and below the setting line are joined, the resulting line that bisects the setting line will be at 90° to it and central (the centre line).

As you lay the points out on the floor, number them with corresponding numbers on the ground plan so that you do not lose count of the co-ordinates.

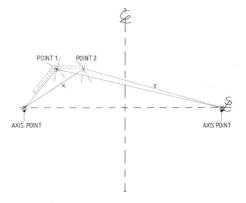

5.3 Marking stage positions

Pinpointing setting co-ordinates can also be done by using the setting and the centre lines. Positions can be established by measuring along the setting line and up or down the centre line. This can be extremely tiresome with large sets and may indeed be inaccurate. It has its uses, however, when marking furniture, as it may be necessary to mark up the furniture in a small rehearsal room where the full extent of the setting line cannot be marked out.

Trace marks should be left for the tab line, iron line, setting line and centre line,

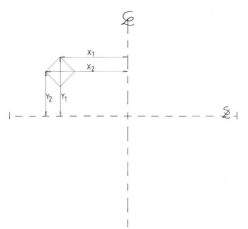

5.4 *Marking furniture positions/stage positions*

for the benefit of both the director and the stage manager. But these should be discrete and should not confuse the actor. For a studio mark-out the parameters of the acting area should be marked up with the front of the stage and entrances in a traditional theatre setting.

The mark-out now complete, you are ready to position the rehearsal furniture which will act as a substitute for the real thing. In many cases the real thing will not be selected until the director and designer have had an opportunity to work with the actor in rehearsal. The rehearsal furniture is important, for it is this that the actors will become accustomed to – if the real thing is totally different and is encountered only in the production week, it can be a real shock to the actor's system. It is prudent, therefore, to select this furniture with care. It should be no more than six inches larger than the real thing and have all the characteristics of the intended piece, i.e. arms on a chair, four legs on a table. Even if it adds to your hire period, it can be worth getting the real thing for the latter part of rehearsal.

Rehearsal props must at this stage be available even if, as usually happens, they are not used for the initial blocking.

These rehearsal props may be crude but they must be comprehensive. A prop list for each act and scene will have been drawn up so that an assessment of cost, complexity and selection can be done. You will not at this point have the setting for all, if any, of these props but that is what the rehearsal is for.

With the director's and stage manager's table positioned in front of the mark-out, the scene is now almost set for the rehearsal, providing the stage manager has all the trappings required to support the needs of the rehearsal. The stage manager's box should include the following for rehearsal:

Practical items:
- First Aid box, including painkillers and tampons
- Clipboard
- Hole punch
- Stapler
- Marking tape (cloth) in various colours
- Stanley knife
- Scissors
- Drawing pins
- Stop watch
- Soap
- Corkscrew
- Lots of pencils
- Erasers
- Pencil sharpener
- Glue for paper
- Superglue (or a strong glue)
- Snap line
- 2 long tape measures 60–100 ft/18.5 to 30.5 metres (cloth)
- 1 short tape measure (steel)
- Highlighter pens
- Chalk
- Flash light
- Coins for telephones

Paperwork
- Call sheets
- Cue sheets, for lights and sound
- Stage plans
- Cast list
- Rehearsal notebook.

THE PROMPT BOOK

For the DSM there now starts the process of creating the prompt book which will become central to the production. In the prompt script will be recorded the actors' moves, technical cues and calls, all relating directly to the text itself. In addition to these the prompt book should contain the points mentioned below:

1 Up-to-date company addresses that include the director, designer, lighting designer, sound designer and stage management team.

2 A provisional prop list that has been drawn up from the text with reference to the director and the designer.

3 A provisional list of lighting cues that have been the basis for initial discussion between the director and the lighting designer.

4 A provisional list of sound cues and effects that have been drawn up after discussion with the sound designer/engineer and the director.

MOVES	CALLS	CUES	
			42 LOOT
			HAL. Anyone can make a mistake.
			TRUSCOTT. Maybe. But he's obviously getting into the habit of making mistakes. Where does he engender these unwanted children? There are no open spaces. The police patrol regularly. It should be next to impossible to commit the smallest act of indecency, let alone beget a child. Where does he do it?
			HAL. On crowded dance floors during the rhumba.
			FAY enters left.
			TRUSCOTT (*removing his pipe, patiently*). I'm a busy man, miss. Do as you're told and wait outside.
			FAY. What's your name?
			TRUSCOTT. I prefer to remain anonymous for the present.
			FAY. Your Christian name.
			TRUSCOTT. I'm not a practising Christian.
			FAY. Is it Jim?
			TRUSCOTT. No.
			FAY. A man at the door says it is.
			TRUSCOTT. I'd like to help him, but I'm not prepared to admit to any name other than my own.
			FAY. He says his name is Meadows.
			TRUSCOTT (*pause, nods his head sagely*). One of my names is Jim. Clearly this fellow is in possession of the fact and wishes to air his knowledge. I shall speak to him.
			TRUSCOTT goes off left.
			FAY (*closing the door, whispers*). There's a uniformed policeman at the door! They're on to us.
			HAL. It's bluff.
			FAY. No. God works for them. They have Him in their pockets like we've always been taught.
			HAL. We've got to get rid of him. He'll find the body next.
			He opens the wardrobe door and puts FAY's shoes and the coathanger inside. He closes the door quickly and turns to FAY.

5.5 Prompt copy layout in prompt script

The creation of a prompt script/book will ensure the centralization of information for the whole of the production. This will mean that the director will only have to go to one source to implement a change in any technical aspect of the production.

There are many ways of making up a prompt script. The most common is to use two copies of the script from which alternate pages are pasted into the loose leaves of an A4 binder. The use of two scripts ensures that the text always remains on the right hand page (see fig. 5:5).

The positioning of the text on the A4 sheet should be such that there is sufficient room between the rings of the binder and the start of the text to write in the cues that relate directly to the script. The opposite page can then be divided centrally into two columns, the left-hand column being devoted to actors' moves and the right-hand column being devoted to actors' calls. The physical compilation of this prompt script should be done well in advance of the first rehearsal.

As already mentioned, it is customary for the first day of rehearsal to be devoted to 'blocking', the process whereby the director takes the cast rapidly through the text giving them their basic moves, including their entrances, exits and onstage positions. Both the DSM and the actors themselves will be required to note these moves – the actors so that they can reproduce these moves the next time they rehearse, the DSM so that s/he can remind the director and cast of the moves that were originally rehearsed. It is helpful if there are copious numbers of pencils and erasers that can be made available to the cast.

The writing of the moves is best done using a series of abbreviations which should be presented at the front of the prompt script. These can form a key – see for example fig. 5:6.

Characters' names are used as it is more than possible that the prompt script may be used in conjunction with another cast.

The stage positions relate to a grid format which gives six stage positions that can be overlaid onto any set (see fig. 5:7), as discussed in Chapter 2.

Moves Shorthand Key	
Mr Higgins	Mr H.
Mrs Higgins	Mrs H.
The Reverend Brown	Rev B.
Colonel Burrows	CB
Vanessa Brown	VB
Clare, the maid	C
Centre stage sofa	Sofa C.S.
Stage left table	Table S.L.
French windows	FW
Up right	USR
Up centre	USC
Up left	USL
Centre right	CSR
Centre stage	CS
Centre left	CSL
Down right	DSR
Down centre	DSC
Down left	DSL
To move	X
To turn	↻
To sit	↓
To rise	↑
To kneel	↘
To enter	ENT
To exit	EXIT

5.6 Prompt script key

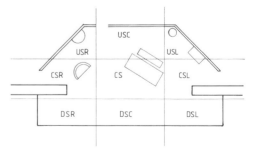

5.7 Grid over stage plan

The stage co-ordinates can be laid on a small-scale drawing denoting the scenery and furniture for each scene. The use of a small template cut from card can save a great deal of time if the drawing needs to be repeated on every page.

The moves themselves are numbered starting from 1 on every new page. The position of the move is marked in the script by using a circled number which corresponds with what is written against that number in the 'moves' column on the far left. The diagram of the set can also be used to mark in the starting positions of each of the characters at the beginning of a scene. When the blocking becomes extremely complex you may even need to mark the characters' positions at the start of every page of the script.

It is wise not to overcomplicate the shorthand used for moves as this can easily lead to confusion when reading them back. If moves are added in later rehearsals then it is a simple job to insert A, B, and C etc. next to the new moves: you don't have to renumber everything on the page. As the blocking continues it is important that you do not allow the pace to overrun your ability to write in the moves. A useful word on these occasions can be 'stop'. There are some directors who take a fiendish delight in watching the DSM's pencil burst into flames!

Even at an early stage in rehearsal actors' calls can start to be pencilled in, which allows you the opportunity to check to see if indeed the actors are standing by to rehearse. If not, you have a written prompt that will send you off to look for them.

As the books go down and the actors start to try and survive without the text in front of them, the gentle process of prompting in rehearsal begins. It is inevitable that actors will first paraphrase the text and occasionally lose their way. It is always worth putting a pencil mark against these parts of the text rather than jumping in at the very moment the lines are being delivered. Where possible you should wait for a brief lull in the rehearsal process to catch up with the actor concerned and correct on a one to one basis. You must not let actors continually get the text wrong without correction for this can lead to the incorrect text being lodged in the actor's memory which can sometimes be impossible to erase.

It is worthwhile timing scenes as they are rehearsed. This can often benefit the director, giving them another perspective on the way in which the scene is being played. It also benefits the DSM for it is useful to note for the technical department how long the time gap is between each cue.

CALLS ON THE CALL BOARD

After the initial blocking the director will go back and start to work through sections of the play with only those present in the scenes attending the rehearsal. It is at this stage that you can use the availability chart that you have drawn up to full advantage.

At the end of the day the director sits down to decide the format of the following day's rehearsal. The order of the scenes and those involved will be listed by the DSM, typed up and posted on the agreed call boards. On some occasions it may be necessary to ring round those members of the company who were not present at the end of rehearsal. If, however, you post a call at the theatre switchboard it is possible for members of the company to ring in for their call. Call sheets should show the date to which the call applies, the show, the venue for rehearsal and the approximate running times of the rehearsal.

MOVES	CALLS
1. TRUS X CSR	
2. FAY ENT SL X DS	
3. TRUS X USC	
4. HAL ↓ SR CHAIR	
5. TRUS X EXIT SL	
6. FAY X SL CLOSE DOOR	
→ X SR CHAIR	
7. HAL ↑ X DSC	

5.8 *Marking in moves*

CUES

42   LOOT

HAL. Anyone can make a mistake.   ①
TRUSCOTT. Maybe. But he's obviously getting into the habit of
  making mistakes. Where does he engender these unwanted
  children? There are no open spaces. The police patrol
  regularly. It should be next to impossible to commit the
  smallest act of indecency, let alone beget a child. Where does
  he do it?
HAL. On crowded dance floors during the rhumba.

② FAY *enters left.*

TRUSCOTT (*removing his pipe, patiently*). I'm a busy man, miss.
  Do as you're told and wait outside.
FAY. What's your name?   ③
TRUSCOTT. I prefer to remain anonymous for the present.
FAY. Your Christian name.
TRUSCOTT. I'm not a practising Christian.
FAY. Is it Jim?
TRUSCOTT. No.
FAY. A man at the door says it is.   ④
TRUSCOTT. I'd like to help him, but I'm not prepared to admit
  to any name other than my own.
FAY. He says his name is Meadows.
TRUSCOTT (*pause, nods his head sagely*). One of my names is
  Jim. Clearly this fellow is in possession of the fact and wishes
  to air his knowledge. I shall speak to him.

⑤   TRUSCOTT *goes off left.*

FAY (*closing the door, whispers*). There's a uniformed police-
⑥ man at the door! They're on to us.
HAL. It's bluff.
FAY. No. God works for them. They have Him in their pockets
  like we've always been taught.
HAL. We've got to get rid of him. He'll find the body next.

⑦ *He opens the wardrobe door and puts* FAY'S *shoes and the
  coathanger inside. He closes the door quickly and turns to* FAY.

Against each time should be given the real names of the actors required and a reference to which part of the play is to be rehearsed. If two people are called for one time and another person is called at a later time to participate in the same scene, 'to join' is written beside the name of the third party scheduled to arrive later. It is extremely important that the cast are aware of which parts of the text are going to be rehearsed, so that they know sections they should concentrate on learning.

The names on the call sheet should be listed alphabetically (and, of course, with the ladies first).

A scene synopsis can be helpful to establish the agreed divisions in the text. If posted on the notice board it can prevent confusion with calls.

```
        THE BUS AND TRUCK THEATRE COMPANY

                    'THE SEA'

   REHEARSAL CALL - FRIDAY 6TH DECEMBER 1996

        AT - THE MEMORIAL HALL, PONTELAND


10.00 AM  -  SCENE ONE   -   ADAM HALL
                             MICHAEL JOHNSON
                             MATTHEW HENSHAW

11.00 AM  -  SCENE TWO   -   LYNNE MARTINDALE
                             BEVERLEY WINN

12.00 PM  -  TO JOIN     -   MATT BOND
                             BEN JAMES
                             RICHARD TIERNEY

1.00 PM   -  LUNCH

2.00 PM   -  SCENE THREE -   ADAM HALL
                             MICHAEL JOHNSON
                             MATTHEW HENSHAW
                             RICHARD TIERNEY

3.30 PM   -  SCENE FOUR  -   LYNNE MARTINDALE
                             NICOLA PHILLIPS
                             JENNY MYLOVE
                             BRITTANY BAINBRIDGE
                             ELAINE MICHAELS
                             BEVERLEY WINN
                             VERNA SMITH
                             THOMAS ALLAN

5.00 PM   -  FINISH

THANK YOU


JOE BLOGGS
STAGE MANAGER
```

5.9 *(a) Rehearsal call*

```
THE BUS AND TRUCK THEATRE COMPANY

           'THE SEA'

      SCENE SYNOPSIS:
```

		PAGE NUMBERS
SCENE ONE:	THE BEACH	1 - 2
SCENE TWO:	THE DRAPER'S SHOP	3 - 11
SCENE THREE:	THE BEACH	11 - 17
SCENE FOUR:	PARK HOUSE	17 - 29
SCENE FIVE:	THE DRAPER'S SHOP	29 - 40
SCENE SIX:	THE BEACH	40 - 46
SCENE SEVEN:	THE CLIFFTOP	47 - 59
SCENE EIGHT:	THE BEACH	60 - 65

5.9 *(b) Scene synopsis*

A cast list should be posted on the board with or before the first call. This cast list should show the understudies if they have been agreed at this point.

'THE SEA'

CAST LIST

IN ORDER OF APPEARANCE

WILLY CARSON	ADAM HALL
EVANS	MATTHEW HENSHAW
HATCH	MICHAEL JOHNSON
HOLLARCUT	RICHARD TIERNEY
VICAR	THOMAS ALLAN
CARTER	MATT BOND
THOMPSON	BEN JAMES
LOUISE RAFI	BEVERLEY WINN
ROSE JONES	JENNY MYLOVE
JESSICA TILEHOUSE	LYNNE MARTINDALE
MAFANWY PRICE	VERNA SMITH
JILLY	ELAINE MICHAELS
RACHEL	NICOLA PHILLIPS
DAVIS	BRITTANY BAINBRIDGE

5.9 *(c) Cast list*

REHEARSAL NOTES

As the rehearsal progresses the complexities of the staging start to develop. To ensure that none of the detail discussed in the rehearsal is lost to those not immediately present there, stage management use a rehearsal notebook, which is generally a carbon copy book, giving one original and one carbon copy of any notes taken. These rehearsal notes will form the bridge between the rehearsal process and the production departments who will provide the lighting, sound, costume and scenery. These departments need to have an up-to-date report of anything that may affect them so that they can adjust, expand or abort the work they currently have in progress. The rehearsal notebook should

have on it, like all the paperwork, the name of the play and the date of the notes.

The notes are an opportunity to cross-check existing information as much as they are to introduce new information. If there is a reference to a prop, the rehearsal note should indicate the act, scene and page number where this prop is used. This also applies to costume, sound and light, of course. The rehearsal notes can almost be regarded as a newsletter from rehearsal.

It is the stage manager's job to distribute the information gained from rehearsal notes to all the relevant departments.

REHEARSAL PROPS

By the time the play has been worked through once the DSM should start to have an idea as to the positioning of the practical props used in the production. It would then be worthwhile to start developing a provisional setting list that can be up-dated over the weeks of rehearsal. The setting list will be an extension of the provisional prop list that was compiled for the initial production meeting. As the rehearsals progress the prop setting needs will increase and the DSM may start to need assistance in rehearsal to keep track of the continual setting and resetting of props. During this time the provisional prop list will develop into the prop setting (see fig. opposite) and running plots. These plots are of key importance during rehearsal. The rehearsal process involves the running and re-running of scenes. The props in these scenes must be therefore set, reset and checked by the stage management. There are other offstage or scene change elements that if required should be included in a running plot. There will, of course, also be the ongoing battle to fit in

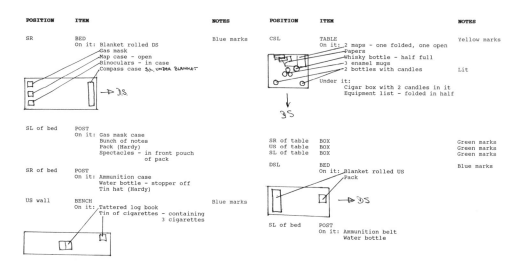

THE BUS AND TRUCK THEATRE COMPANY

'JOURNEY'S END

PROP SETTING LIST

POSITION	ITEM	NOTES
SR	BED On it: Blanket rolled DS Gas mask Map case - open Binoculars - in case Compass case SL UNDER BLANKET	Blue marks
SL of bed	POST On it: Gas mask case Bunch of notes Pack (Hardy) Spectacles - in front pouch of pack	
SR of bed	POST On it: Ammunition case Water bottle - stopper off Tin hat (Hardy)	
US wall	BENCH On it: Tattered log book Tin of cigarettes - containing 3 cigarettes	Blue marks

POSITION	ITEM	NOTES
CSL	TABLE On it: 2 maps - one folded, one open Papers Whisky bottle - half full 3 enamel mugs 2 bottles with candles	Yellow marks Lit
	Under it: Cigar box with 2 candles in it Equipment list - folded in half	
SR of table	BOX	Green marks
US of table	BOX	Green marks
SL of table	BOX	Green marks
DSL	BED On it: Blanket rolled US Pack	Blue marks
SL of bed	POST On it: Ammunition belt Water bottle	

5.10 Prop setting list

wardrobe calls while still maintaining a balanced rehearsal schedule.

The DSM will also be required to provide live effects such as buzzers and bells, but if the sound is more complicated than this, the sound department may need to be in attendance.

As the production week approaches the director will run the play more and more often, giving the cast more of an opportunity to pace themselves and develop light and shade across the whole of their performance.

Pre-production Checklist

- Copyright clearance of the play

- Confirmation of performance days and venues

- Bar licence application (for Green Room or indeed FOH)

- Production meeting: discuss concept and design

- Organize auditions, space, staffing and auditionees

- Reading and working copies of the play for staff and cast

- Production meeting: discuss practical staging requirements

- Agree budget of play with director, production manager etc

- Draw up production schedule

- Draw up detailed staffing requirements and action

- Organize rehearsal space

- Mail-out to cast prior to first reading, to include call sheet and script

- Research play's period, style and text

- Provisional prop list, costume plot, lighting plot, and sound plot to be in hand

- Duplication of ground plans and distribution to technical departments

- Production meeting

- Call all available production staff for first reading

- Make application for special licences: children, firearms, exotic animals, fire

- Organization of specialist skills: fight directors, choreographers, vocal coaching, musical direction, or whatever!

- Completion of construction drawings.

- First reading

- Mark-out of rehearsal space

- First rehearsal

- Establish regular production meetings

- Ongoing prop research

- Ongoing prop finding with design

- Costume fittings and wig fittings

- Monitor overall hours of company

- Set building is ongoing

- Supply of programme information including cast, staff and credits

- Photo-call organization

- Timings to FOH and Management

- Organization of complimentary tickets and free programmes

- Follow through of specialist licences

- Brief summary of play to box office

- Development of flying plot

- Detailed planning of scene changes

- Development of show running plots

- Show staffing

- Detailed prop setting lists from rehearsal

- Programme proofing

- Dressing room list

- Costume parade list

- Prop parade

- Photo-call shot list

6. The Production Week

The term 'production week' is used here to mean the period of time that is available to 'get in' to your venue and conduct the last technical and dress rehearsals. In some amateur situations it may be that you do not have access to the venue all the time. I have, for the purpose of the hypothetical production schedule which follows, assumed that there will be virtual limitless access to the venue over the course of three days. You will find that the purpose of each element of the production schedule does not change even though the time allotted may be somewhat different. I have therefore through the course of this chapter outlined the most preferable working situation.

During this time a stage manager will be required to integrate the often contradictory requirements of each department. Lighting staff will want darkness to focus the lighting rig, scenic artists need light to touch up the set, the stage floor needs repainting and the flyman needs to set deads, the combinations are endless.

In this day and age we are used to the concept of multi tasking computers, stage managers have been doing this for years. The production week is the period when they must be able to fully exercise this skill. Managing your time and the time of others requires you to be realistic, focused and a good listener but not a 'yes' person.

With some people the enormity of the task causes them to overestimate the length of time they need. In others the desire to please or ill-founded confidence causes an under estimation of the time needed. Both need to be identified and readjusted.

In short an ability to spot the difference between a request for additional time that is a real need and those which are indulging in a bit of 'rump' covering is a key part of the process. Your job is to get the cast on stage on schedule with all the elements of the production in place.

Negotiating the give and take between departments will never be resolved if it is allowed to escalate to confrontation. For this reason never let your sense for humour submerge under pressure.

The production week is the point where everything that has been worked out on paper comes to fruition in practice. The paper calculations do not always produce the anticipated practical answer. So there has to be a margin of flexibility in any schedule and a margin of compromise in any answer to a problem. It is the stage manager's duty to ensure that these margins are kept to an absolute minimum. People's tempers will fray and their sense of humour will fail but you must continually remind yourself that you are all working together, hopefully as a team, and certainly to the same end.

See our imaginary production week schedules opposite.

Any schedule must reflect the time available and the work that realistically has to be done. Lunch breaks, and resetting time for props and wardrobe must be allowed for – so should opportunities for technical adjustments that may require stage access. You must discuss all aspects of a schedule with the heads of department involved when it is initially created, and you must be ready to evaluate progress at every stage of production.

SUNDAY

8 am	Get-in of scenery, costumes, lighting, sound, props. Commence rigging, lighting, sound and masking.
10 am	Start building scenic elements.
1 pm	Costume parade on stage. Lunch break. Electrics, sound and carpenters.
2 pm	Continue build and rigging.
4 pm	Focusing lights.
6.30 pm	Supper break. Carpenters and sound. Continue focusing.
7.30 pm	Sound rehearsal. Supper break. Electrics. Scenic finish and tidy.
8.30 pm	Lighting session commences.
12 pm	Finish.

MONDAY

8 am	Technical checks.
9 am	Commence stopping dress rehearsal Part 1.
1 pm	Lunch break.
2 pm	Technical adjustments.
2.30 pm	Commence stopping dress rehearsal Part 2.
6.30 pm	Supper break for cast. Reset of staging, props etc.
7.30 pm	Supper break for stage management, lighting, sound.
8.30 pm	Commence first dress rehearsal.
11.30 pm	Finish.

TUESDAY

9 am	Technical adjustments as required. Reset.
10 am	Cast notes from director.
12 am	Lunch break.
1.25 pm	Half-hour call for second dress rehearsal.
2 pm	Second dress rehearsal.
5 pm	Finish second dress rehearsal. Cast notes from director. Reset.
5.45 pm	Supper break.
6.55 pm	Half hour call for 7.30 curtain.
7.30 pm	First performance.
10.30 pm	Finish.

7. The Get-in and Fit-up

The get-in is an extremely important part of the whole production process for any time lost here will be doubly paid for later when the full company are in attendance. When touring, the time given for a get-in is very often less than is allowed for in a normal situation (if such a thing exists) but the principles are still the same.

The get-in is the point at which the scenery and associated equipment (costumes, props, lighting) are brought into the theatre/venue and positioned ready for use. At this time it is important the stage manager ensures that all the scenery and equipment are positioned so that they are readily available for when the fit-up begins. If it becomes necessary to double handle all the scenery while digging out the relevant pieces you will risk a delay in the schedule and a loss of credibility with the crew. So ensure that the items you will need first are easily accessible. If scenery and equipment are not positioned properly in the first place it will just cause delay or damage later. If space is tight it is better to get costume racks, baskets and driers up to wardrobe as soon as possible rather than leave them lying around. This must also apply to props, including furniture, which should be placed somewhere safe such as the back of the auditorium, until they are needed. Make sure props are covered to stop people using them.

A stage manager should not be found at the doors of the truck or in the depths of the wardrobe during the get-in. He/she should be positioned on stage to direct the positioning of equipment and scenery and be available to answer questions. It is very often useful to have a table downstage centre where the plans of the theatre and the construction drawings can be laid out to allow easy reference. It will of course be necessary to mark up the stage prior to the get-in to allow for the selection of flying bars and positioning of the set. Get there early! Your knowledge of the theatre/venue will be the key to the smooth running of the get-in and fit-up.

It may be advantageous to stagger the process of getting-in when there is a large amount of equipment and scenery, bringing in electrics and sound first, then staging, followed by scenery. This can prevent your ending up with a great pile of stuff in the middle of the very stage you wish to work on. The use of a get-in crew (they have the unfortunate name of humpers) whose sole function is to fetch and carry can save the energy of those who will have to work on and it allows your crew to start work the moment the kit is through the get-in doors. Traditionally, the get-in crew are paid a fixed amount that covers the get-in (and the get-out when on tour) which used to be negotiated prior to anything moving and are paid cash in hand at the end of the production. Nowadays, however, the payment is based on an hourly rather than a negotiated rate and is not so often paid in cash due to the administrative problems this gives rise to and government tax departments.

How long will a get-in take? The show

has to be got into the theatre from either the workshop or through the get-in doors. A team of humpers might empty a 40 ft articulated trailer in half an hour with a relatively short and easy get-in route. This however does not necessarily give enough time for the appropriate positioning of each piece of equipment and scenery and avoid time lost through double handling of scenery and equipment. You could therefore allow an hour at least for an easy show and up to as much as six hours for a staggered, complex get-in that merges into the fit-up. In winter everyone may benefit from a quick get-in just to get the dock doors shut. Also in winter, or at night, liaise with the electrics department to provide some lights on stands outside so that you can see what is in the truck.

With any set it is important to ensure that all flying and lighting rigging over the stage is done as soon as is possible that is :

- Lx bars
- borders
- legs
- flown scenery

When touring this involves getting electrics and any flown pieces in first. The flying plot or rigging plot for the suspension of masking, lighting and scenery should have been agreed well in advance so that the correct bars have been cleared of any accessories on the get-out of the last show. This should allow the combined hanging of lighting and masking. When flying large pieces, it can be useful to hang them earlier rather than later for as they go up they can swing and strike the surrounding bars, and if these are electric bars you could find yourself going to the bottom of the popularity chart!

If a stage cloth is being used now is the time to lay it before the stage gets full of rubbish, although the stage should always be swept before a stage cloth goes down. It should be swept downstage to upstage for the benefit of the FOH Manager. Whether a stage cloth or a stage floor is used, a certain amount of marking out has to go on to ensure that the set ends up in the right place.

While this is going on other members of the team are hanging up the costumes in the pre-arranged dressing rooms and creating a company office. When the main fabric of the set is together the stage management team should establish prop tables left and right and agree the siting of the prompt corner, checking that the sightlines are as good as they can be.

This period can very often produce some frayed tempers for everyone is trying to get on – your ability to manage the people and the inanimate objects with equal skill will truly be tested here. In a situation such as this, do not try to make a decision for the heads of department, make them make it. If there are particularly sensitive problems try and make the decision with the HODs before you get on stage and make people stick to them. Procrastination in a production meeting will only lead to a protracted problem on site, whereas if a controlled decision has already been made then it is always possible to change it later.

THE FIT-UP

The fit-up is the direct follow through of the get-in and they are in effect seamless but for the tea break that usually comes after a large get-in. This break is a great opportunity to have a relaxed strategy chat with the HODs to agree on the order of play for the rest of the day. As your staff will be dispersed throughout the building, it is important that you create and use opportunities where all the principal members of staff can discuss minor problems and details of scheduling. They should all have a comprehensive schedule at this point but it is unadvisable, nay impossible, to schedule every detail.

Stage managers may on some occasions have to flex their psychic powers but they should not ask this of others. A flyman stuck 30 ft above the stage with yesterday's copy of the local paper or another sort of pictorial diversion needs to know what is going on in some detail to allow him to get organized and so avoid delay. Flymen as a breed are very philosophical. In many cases they have watched the world go by from their fly door above the stage for many years – they have seen it all before, and will just wait for you to get yourself organized. Because of this they often need motivating and the best motivational force will be your understanding of their needs and your ability to convey your needs too. Enough said, the flyman's situation is in many ways a prime example of the sort of communication problem you may encounter in some form or another in all departments – wardrobe at the top of the dressing room stairs, electrics control at the back of the auditorium, sound control at the back of the stalls, crew room understage, they all have to know what is going on. Walkie talkies can assist in this communication. They are not well suited to discussion as they are public, noisy and more at home with security guards. Given this they can be useful for giving directions to lighting crew who are on the move focusing lanterns or flymen working on the grid. They can also be useful for ASMs who may be running round the theatre doing the myriad of things that need to be done at this stage in production.

In the production week, and potentially in performance, the use of a multi channel ring intercom can allow the allocation of channels to individual departments, such as; one for SM, one for Lx and maybe another for stage floor and flys (especially during the technical and dress rehearsals). Multi channel rings can prevent confusion in performance on shows where the flies and the stage floor need to communicate for scene changes or follow spot operators need to talk to each other to synchronise actions. While on separate rings the users can hear the DSM and switch on to the SM ring to acknowledge instructions and standbys. Ring intercoms usually take the form of single ear muff headsets with a boom microphone and are hard wired via a switched belt pack into a connection box on a wall. They can however also be used in conjunction with a radio loop to allow users to move around without being plugged into the wall.

It is important to establish who needs what in the way of paperwork at an early stage in the production process. It is seldom a good idea to give everybody everything as people are unable to extract the information relevant to their department. For the get-in and fit-up here is a guide as to who needs what. The stage and production managers will need a full set of each.

Production schedule – *for all heads of department and notice board*

Working drawings – *for master carpenter*

Stage plan (showing staging) – *all heads of department*

Stage plan (showing flying) – *for master carpenter and Lx head of department and head flyman*

Staging and flying detail – *for head flyman*

Stage elevation/section (showing staging, lighting bars, borders and flown pieces) – *for all heads of department*

Dressing room list – *for notice board and wardrobe department*

Flying chart – *Lx head of department, master carpenter and head flyman*

Cast list – *wardrobe department and notice board*

Lx working light requirement – *for Lx department*

List of Lx cues – *for Lx department*

List of flying cues – *for head flyman*

List of sound cues – *for sound department*

(Detailed show running information is not essential, as crew will only lose anything you give them at this stage.)

The fit-up is essentially the hanging of masking, lights and scenery, the laying of stage surfaces and the construction of the set. During the fit-up the stage manager will mark out the key co-ordinates on to the stage using the same method as for rehearsal mark-out. More time has been wasted through the incorrect positioning of staging, lighting and furniture than will ever be admitted to.

The stage manager should be continually conscious of positioning, the butting of flats, good joins, bad joins and will also generally monitor progress. But a good stage manager should not be found at the top of a ladder or any similar place, for there may well be three people at the bottom of the ladder waiting for the answer to a question without which they cannot continue. Most designers will have a major input at this stage if it is a new production, but if you are on tour you are on your own.

Breaks are important for the crew and they will look to the stage manager to call them – but if you misjudge or forget to call a break due to your excessive enthusiasm you will find the crew slowly drifting off. The stage manager should also be thinking ahead, for if the tea urn is empty at

break time there is precious little point in stopping. I have always found that bacon and egg sandwiches have a profound effect on a crew after an early morning get-in. If you can organize *this* effectively most crews will feel that you can organize most things – if you are in a foreign town they may well be right!

Staggering breaks can also be effective, giving the Lx crew an extra hour of darkness for focusing, or perhaps an hour of silence for the sound crew to test levels during which time the design team might like to touch up the set. However you choose to plan it, though, people must have breaks and you must make them take the break provided, for later on in the day when they are tired they may well feel that it was because of you that they did not have one. *If you call a break make sure that everyone knows about it* – tell all HODs and call it over the tannoy or 'voice of God' microphone. Many a flyman has leant over the flyrail as everyone was coming back from a break and asked 'Any chance of a tea break?'

Flooring

If a wooden floor is to be laid during the fit-up, the stage manager should ensure that it has been well filled, sanded, painted and sealed before it goes down. Time will be short during the production process to allow more than just touching up. If the floor itself has to be painted (or repainted) black during the production week then this process must be carefully scheduled. Whether a floor is to be laid or painted, time must be allowed to do the job effectively and also to re-mark the stage for furniture and scenery.

The durability of any stage floor must be carefully considered: a white marble-effect floor may be a wonderful idea, but after two weeks' hard wear will it still be the floor that the designer wanted? If it is sealed well enough to prevent marking, will it be the kind of floor that the dancers will be able to dance on without twisting their ankles?

Floors are always a bone of contention. Dance floor, a relatively pliant lino-type product, is great as long as it is laid on a smooth solid surface and given time to 'lie down' and its seams can be effectively joined with carpet tape. The use of powdered rosin provided backstage in wooden trays can often help with slippery floors. You can 'cake' the floor by applying liberal amounts of Coca Cola and then allowing it to dry, but this is really only for use as a very last resort. An overly zealous cleaning or sealing of the stage by the stage manager can often lead to disasters for both actors and dancers – so be careful, but keep the stage clean. As I mentioned before, stages are traditionally swept downstage to upstage to prevent the dust and rubbish being brushed into the auditorium. It is cheaper to clean the stage rather than the velvet of the seats and it can also prevent the wrath of the FOH manager from descending upon you. A sprinkling of water and/or rough sawdust can prevent the sweeper disappearing in a cloud of dust and choking the crew.

One kind of floor covering most commonly found in opera, is a 'floor cloth'. This is wedged into a cloth trap at the front of the stage on the tab line and 'kicked out' upstage by crew (with plimsolls on), then tacked on the upstage edge to hold it in position. This allows a complex floor design to be made on soft cloth that can be easily folded or rolled and stored, and reused with relative ease.

Rugs and carpets of any description must be well secured, tacked or stuck with webbing based double-sided tape to ensure they do not curl and cause an actor to trip. If a rug is to be laid in a scene change it is best, if possible, to secure it firmly with heavy furniture to prevent it from moving.

AND ON . . .

As the fit-up continues the stage management team will be required to position the set dressing and furniture, in conjunction with the designer. The final position of the furniture will be decided in conjunction with the director and principal actors; the final position of the dressing may have to be agreed with the designer as the fit-up continues.

The set dressing, which may be items on a mantelpiece, pictures and other static items, will in some cases need to be stuck down. Flexible adhesive, double-sided tape and a staple gun can at this stage be very useful. Pictures that leap off the wall every time a door is shut are very unconvincing. This is the time to position off stage prop tables and props but beware that you do not set the practical props too early and expose them to possible damage.

As the set goes up lanterns will be rigged and flashed through to ensure that they work before proceeding. Initially they will not have been focused on a specific spot for this will require a degree of darkness which, to my mind, most lighting designers are born screaming for. Because the Lx department needs darkness they may well reach a point where they cannot continue without it and therefore reach a hiatus. It is at this stage that they may be able to wire up a practical lamp or position the backstage workers and cue lights that you requested in writing over a week earlier. It is, however, often quite possible to focus some of the lights in a limited amount of working light, though this inevitably means that the technicians will have to go back and tweak them at a later stage. It is at this point that people will often switch off working lights (often called 'workers') without warning. This should never be done – those at the top of a ladder with a nail in one hand and a hammer in the other will fail to see the potentially funny side of the situation and it is, of course, dangerous.

To focus effectively, the lighting designer will need near complete darkness, and all the relevant furniture and scenery on its marks for each scene or act. The production desk should be positioned centrally in the stalls area to allow an overall view of the stage. It should also have headphones/intercom stations for the lighting designer, the DSM, SM/Production manager and if needs be the director (though I think it is better without the director 'on cans'). The staff working at the desk will also require dimmable working lights together with a continually live 'voice of God' microphone, which can be switched on to allow instant access to all ears in the theatre. The production desk will not necessarily be used at this stage by the lighting designer for he/she may well use the downstage centre table to work from, allowing easy access to plans and lights simultaneously. But it is usually best to position the production desk before the lights go out. Prior to focusing, the stage manager must ensure that all furniture positions, scenic positions and flying deads are set for a lantern focus, as an undeaded flying piece is just a time waster. It can so often happen that the lighting designer spends ten minutes pointing a light only to discover that it is not on its pre-arranged position.

During focusing there will be a junior board operator on the lighting desk and electricians up ladders, on bridges, focusing lanterns under the direction of the lighting designer who usually stands on the stage. The relationship between light-

ing designer and those at the top of the ladder is unique – many lighting designers have favourite lighting technicians with whom they share a level of technical understanding and a degree of telepathy. This, combined with the use of short-range unlicensed walky talkies, reduces the time needed for adjusting each lens, shutter, iris, barndoor and lamp, to say nothing of the cutting of colour and its insertion into frames and lanterns.

At this stage the lighting designer will want to check the furniture positions, actors' moves and actors' specials with stage management so it can be useful to have someone from the team available. When the focusing and the set is complete it is time to sit down with the director, designer, lighting designer, stage managers and DSM and light the play.

THE LIGHTING SESSION

The lighting session is the process whereby having allocated each lantern in the rig an area of the stage to light, they are selectively combined to give an overall effect. The initial effect is created by the lighting designer, who puts together a combination of lanterns to form a lighting state. This is not, as it may at first seem, a random operation but a carefully planned exercise by the lighting designer involving the creation of a number of rigging plans. The lighting designer will communicate to the board operator, if possible via an intercom, the numbers of the circuits he/she requires and the level of intensity at which they are needed. When the lighting designer feels that the effect has been achieved, a 'walker' will be called upon to strut across the stage so that those sat around the production desk can see the effect the light may have on the actors. Walkers are very often members of the stage management team or others volunteered by the stage manager. They should, when possible, have on the sort of colours worn by the actors. If the play is a Restoration comedy, then a dress coat may be a suitable item to wear giving a visual guide to those seeing the scene for the first time. This is very often when discussion starts between director and both designers as to the effectiveness of what they are seeing.

During the lighting process each cue will be gone through systematically, starting with house lights and preset lighting on the set if tabs are not used. The lighting designer and director will both have a typed-up list of cues provided by the stage management team which has been drawn from the rehearsals, and agreed before-hand with the director. This list of cues will have formed the basis of a number of discussions between the designer, director and lighting designer when the objective and action of each cue will have been discussed in detail, any changes and developments that have occurred having been relayed to the lighting department. Any lighting designer worth his (or her) salt will attend a number of rehearsals and run-throughs to establish a full working knowledge of the play and the way it is to be performed.

While the lighting session is in progress, the DSM will mark in the text the position of the 'standbys' and 'goes' for each cue, indicating the speed and effect of the cue as it is agreed. (The DSM will already have these cues pencilled in the

---

Lighting Session Checklist

- Establish stalls production desk with controlled lights

- Ensure headsets have been laid out on the production desk and tested

- Clear stage of production bric-a-brac

- Check that all the working lights are off; check the blackout

- Check the set is as it should be for the start of the show: door, windows, furniture? (Sometimes a lighting session is done backwards so that the first set is ready for the technical rehearsal.)

- Ensure that all auditorium doors are closed

- Ensure that the walkers are wearing the right clothes

- Check all the set furniture on the right marks. Mark all furniture once it is lit in position

- See that all members of staff are present: director, lighting designer, set designer, SM/DSM and have an up-to-date list of states and cues

- No refreshments of any kind to be allowed on stage from this point

prompt book, for they will have been called or at least marked in rehearsal.) At this stage the director will very often be looking for confirmation about details of action from the DSM and reminders of what passed in rehearsal, and it is useful for the DSM to sit with the director on one side and lighting designer on the other. As each cue is plotted (agreed) and logged by the board operator – if the board is manual rather than computer logged this can take time – the cue number is confirmed and the cue is operated just to make sure that the timing and effect is that which was originally agreed upon.

This process should be gone through for every single cue in the play, from house lights to the state for the curtain calls and house lights.

The lighting session offers the stage management team an opportunity to set props in the wings which until now it has been unadvisable to do because of too much movement backstage. The lighting session can also give an opportunity to rehearse scene changes but this should only happen if the changes are not complex or don't intrude on the process of lighting the play.

SOUND REHEARSAL

The importance of sound has grown over the years, and this growth has been commensurate with the electronic advances in the field. It is more and more the case that sound operators work from the auditorium without any barrier between them and the sound they are making.

It will be necessary to set the levels of sound and tweak the equalization (tone) to create maximum effect. In a musical this will be an ongoing business but even the smallest sound requirement will need rehearsal prior to the technical rehearsal.

If the sound is wrong or too loud, everyone will hear it and it will not inspire confidence. To give a true rendering of sound quality it is important that the scenery and drapes are in position, for these will affect the acoustic quality of the stage. The onstage speakers should be in their agreed positions and drawn on to the general plan.

Initially the sound engineer will probably wish to balance the system, an antisocial business at the best of times. This involves putting various frequencies through the system to set levels on the sound desk and balance the venue response to certain frequencies, electronically boosting and reducing them to give a true sound. It is better to get this out of the way before calling the director to set levels and check the duration and position of the sounds.

At the rehearsal the director and the DSM will sit at the production desk and as each cue is operated a sound level will be set. The level and quality of the sound must be checked in all areas of the auditorium to ensure that all members of the audience have the full benefit of the effect being played or operated. The DSM will check these cues with 'the book' and pencil in the duration of each effect against the cues that have already been marked in the text.

The electronic reproduction of effects is now so sophisticated that the need for live effects has diminished – but there is still sometimes a place for the live effect. A gunshot tape is rarely effective and thunder from a steel thunder sheet has a presence that is hard to beat. In general it is the more immediate effects that respond well to the use of a live effect, such as those illustrated in 7.1(a) – (f).

The taping, editing and replaying of sound effects is still usually done on a ¼ inch ferrous oxide tape played at 15 or 7½

IPS (inches per second). The replaying of these effects will be poor if the material is not recorded well in the first place and is played back on a low quality system. With the advent of digital systems sound quality has now reached a new high. Digital technology also allows effects to be edited and manipulated to such an extent that virtually anything is possible if the budget is available. There are many specialist sound companies who cater for the theatre, and amateur and professional companies alike should seek specialist help in this area wherever possible.

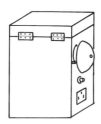

7.1 (a) Bell box

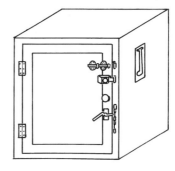

7.1 (d) Door slam

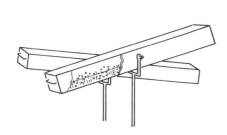

7.1 (b) Rain boxes

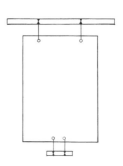

7.1 (e) Thunder sheet

7.1 (c) Glass smash

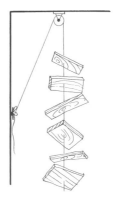

7.1 (f) Clatter crash

8. *In Production*

THE DRESS PARADE

Having built the set, plotted the lighting and sound, it is now time to introduce the acting company to the environment you have created. The first opportunity for this to happen may be the dress parade.

A dress parade may not always take the form of a staged event as I am about to describe but a review of costumes will take place at a relatively late stage in the production process to ensure that all costumes are complete, and have design continuity. The dress parade represents an opportunity to check details with the director, designer, wardrobe mistress/master and most importantly the actor, all of whom should be present to agree the positioning of a handkerchief or the a hat. The more detail that is agreed at an early stage the smoother things will be at the dress rehearsal stage.

There are many advantages of having this costume review on the stage and if at all possible it should be held there. One of the best scheduling opportunities that presents itself is on the first day of a three day production period. At this point the set is up, the lighting positions have been established and rigged, but not all focused, and the crew have gone for a break. By prior arrangement with the lighting designer a few spots can be focused on a pre-arranged downstage area which the stage manager can mark with an X. This will allow the costumes to be seen in a light that is representative of the stage lighting to be used if not the actual light to be used in performance. It is important that the costumes are seen in stage light for it has a different colour temperature from the domestic light found in the wardrobe department. It is also helpful if the lighting designer can supply a little bit of set wash, if this is appropriate, so that the director or designer will also have an opportunity to see the costume in context. At this point, it must be pointed out to the cast that this is not the light for the play but just a staged review of the costumes, predominantly for their benefit. The dress parade is not held so the cast can walk the set poking, prying and criticising, which would be both premature, and extremely irritating for all concerned. In truth, this does not happen for the costumes are extremely important to all concerned and everyone gets on with the job in hand.

With the conventional position of the stalls and a raised stage the audience can have a less than modest view of an actress; they are also in a good position to see the new soles on shoes which a character should have been wearing for years (or indeed witness the cardinal sin, that Mr X actually bought his shoes from Dolcis at a price of £24.99!). All these things should be checked with the actor standing, sitting and lying down, if the text requires it. But this cannot be done if the stage manager has not anticipated the need for a clean cloth for the actor to lie on, a chair to sit on, and a chair on which to place discarded items of clothes. All relevant personal props should be available for this costume review, such as walking sticks, parasols, glasses and their cases (pocket size) handkerchiefs (pocket size in the right colour), cigarette cases/packets, lighters (pocket size), swords etc.

Ten minutes before you think you will be ready to start, ask the company to stand by on the tannoy with 'Ladies and gentlemen this is your five minute call', and repeat. Then three minutes before you think that you will be ready to get going, call the first pair of actors to the wings: 'Mr Jones and Mr Green, this is your call for the dress parade', and repeat. To save time it is important that there is always an actor in the wings ready. So this is possible, call the *next* pair of actors as the second of the *first* pair goes on stage.

A costume review with light, set and staging can only be regarded as the best option, and will not always be possible or desirable. There are a number of factors to take into account: scheduling, the complexity of the show and the period in which it is set, the numbers of the cast. A costume review is often a very difficult experience for the actor to cope with; it is a sensitive matter and it may well not be a good idea for the cast to go through a public appraisal of their costumes. Sometimes this will be unavoidable but it should always be handled with delicacy and tact. However, the dress parade has to happen in one form or another whether it takes place in the wardrobe department itself or a rehearsal room, a dressing room or a stage and it is of vital importance.

This brings me to acknowledge one of the most important performance departments: wardrobe. As they drift from one dressing room to another its members don a large mantle of responsibility. The ward-robe department as a whole are closest to actors in performance; the hours of waiting in dressing rooms and green room lead to long and, in many cases, lasting relationships with actors and actresses. They are in a position to smooth a furrowed brow or a ruffled ego in a way that so often only an experienced company manager is able to do. This relationship can also extend to the dressers, who have a key role to play. A dresser is a particular type of person who is able to work very closely with an actor (clothes on or off!). He/she will understand the insecurities of an actor, giving them confidence in their appearance and a certainty that their costume and personal props will be in order. Through the good offices of a dresser the right things will be washed and pressed to the correct specification and personal props will miraculously appear in the correct pocket of the right suit. Together actor and dresser will achieve the impossible; in small prefabricated quick change booths, on stage or through painstaking rehearsal and preparation they will be able to perform the most fantastic transformations. This can only be done if the stage manager acknowledges and provides for their needs.

A quick change booth is usually constructed with three sides of a square of flattage and a curtain on the fourth side. This provides a discreet space in which the actor can change in a reasonable amount of light (for the light does not spill on the stage). Inside this cubicle the floor should ideally be carpeted, with two hanging racks for the old and new costume, a light, mirror and a table. Sometimes an actor must survive a quick change on his own but will still need the right sort of space.

Occasionally there is not enough time to get to a booth and at this point, a change must take place just off stage. The actor will rely on the stage manager's

Dress Parade Checklist

- Agree running order with wardrobe well in advance and post on call board

- Distribute personal props

- Check the tannoy is switched on and tested

- Electricians should supply an adequate amount of light for the costumes to be seen centre-stage. Mark this point with a cross so that all the actors know where they are well lit. (Worker lights off.)

- Supply a chair for the actors to sit on just upstage of the cross. Another chair can be put to one side on which the actors can lay coats and hats if the dresser is not available

- Ensure there is some easy method by which people can come up on to the stage from the auditorium

- Clear an unobstructed path between the stage door and the stage, free from cables, lamps, ladders etc

- Make the ten and then three minute calls

- Inform the company if there are delays before the start of the dress parade

- Members of staff present should be front of house, director, designer and wardrobe supervisor

- Collect personal props

ability to keep the wings free of any stray onlookers! And the stage manager will, of course, occasionally police the area.

PHOTO CALLS

At some stage in the production process there will be a need for a photo call and this will have to be scheduled very carefully as they are not always as simple as they seem. The photographic session will involve all departments except sound. The costume, props and scenery must all be in place for each shot and the lighting designer must liaise with the photographer to ensure that both photographic and theatrical needs are catered for.

A list of shots should be drawn up with the director, covering all the highlights of the play and including character shots of all the principal players. This list is then posted as a call on the board for the actors, stating the act and scene, with a list of the people involved in each picture. Before compiling the list it may well be a good idea to discuss it with the wardrobe department, who may suggest photographing the play out of sequence to allow time for costume and wig changes. But of course this must be scenically possible and there is no point in implementing it if the actors then have to stand around waiting for their scenery to be set.

Having made certain which props are available, the stage manager will agree the final order of play. Passages of text that lead into the photographic subjects will then be selected so that the DSM give the actors a point to go from. It is very common for posed shots to be taken at a photocall, as this is less likely to be disadvantageous for the actor.

If the session is a press call then it helps to have a list of the scenes presented and those involved, giving their character's name and their own name, so that there is no confusion. If individual leading actor shots are to be given then it is important that the director/producer gives you a policy to follow and for these shots to be organised so as to prevent the whole cast sitting around waiting while they are taken. (Be assured, however, that the press usually get what they want despite your planning.) Production photos (but certainly not the press photographs) can be taken during a dress rehearsal; as flash is so rarely needed in this age of fast film photography it does not usually disrupt the rehearsal. If you are having photographs taken during the dress you must ensure that the cast and wardrobe are informed. If by some unfortunate chance there is an element of the staging or costume that is not yet ready, you must talk it through with the photographer concerned to ensure that he does not waste time on this or make the actors feel uncomfortable.

PROP SETTING

Prop setting is an integral part of the job of stage management. It requires attention to detail that would not be out of place in a hospital and the implementation of basic systems that will cover and correct inevitable human failings.

Furniture must be set on the marks on the floor which were agreed and positioned during rehearsal and the lighting session. On stage, hand props must be in the same place and take the same form every night, so that the actor is completely familiar with them.

Props must be reliable and user-friendly if they are to be truly effective, as they are used repetitively and in the same way by the same nervous actor and nobody wants to increase the chance of something going wrong. It can also be said that in some cases the 'real' props can enhance a performance enormously; Stanislavski's theory that using hot tea in the teapot gives actors a true sense of what they are doing brought a new dimension to properties. However, doors are rarely set in brick walls on stage – and the illusion of the theatre in many cases begins with door acting.

There are many ways in which you can simplify the use of practical objects in a play and avoid problems. The tray of coffee that is brought in may only have coloured card inside the cups, so there won't be any spillage. Matches may be set lid down between the box tray and the open ends of the box casing. The actor therefore is no longer required to open the box as the preset matches are easily pulled out. This prevents the matches dropping out when the box is inadvertently opened the wrong way up. Most of these precautions are common sense but are all part of the process of problem analysis. It is best though to check during the rehearsal process if it's allowable to take these kind of precautions, for you may find the director requesting the props that will directly stimulate a certain aspect of an actor's performance.

Prop tables should be neatly laid out, well lit and in a position where they will be directly accessible to the stage. It can often be a help to attach a large piece of paper onto the table where you can draw the position in which a prop is set and its name. This can act as an instant reminder when setting props. Walking sticks and umbrellas can be placed in a cardboard tube taped to the leg of the table (if they are placed on the table they are liable to roll off).

8.1 Prop table

Whatever the props are, provision must be made to ensure that they are maintained and correctly set out before every performance. The maintenance and refurbishment of props is essential if the quality of a production is to be maintained. The stage manager must ensure that the impetus of the first night is not lost as the run progresses and provision must be made for those items that must look new every night – again, forward planning. Something as simple as ironing sheets for a bed, a tablecloth or handkerchief can have a direct effect on the actor's perfor-

mance, which in turn will influence the audience's perception of the staging of the play.

The setting of props is usually carried out by the ASMs during the day, prior to the performance and it can be done in two parts. First the reset: this is when all the items used are returned to their starting positions for the play. Second, a prop check which comes just before the performance. It is always useful to check the props to a fixed pattern, such as clockwise stage right to stage left, using a setting list of props on which you can tick off each item as it is positioned and checked. If a prop has a practical function then this should be checked at the same time, i.e. if a book is to be opened, open it when checking the props to see if there is any damage.

A prop setting list must detail the positioning of a prop and how it should look, for example, piano – lid open, curtains – closed, tumbler of water – half full (see page 72). A diagram accompanying each list of items can assist enormously with accurate prop setting. If a member of the team is run down by a bus the setting lists should provide enough information for all the props to be set perfectly by another member of the stage management team!

BACKSTAGE ORGANIZATION

A number of aspects of staging a play do not immediately spring to mind when scenic, sound and lighting practicalities are first discussed. The backstage area has to be serviced with the same amount of care and attention to detail as is given to the onstage setting.

All the scenery used requires support of some kind. This may take the form of a stage brace, a French brace or scenic returns on a single flat. A stage brace must be properly keyed in to the screw-eye in the back of a flat to allow no room for movement. The weights and the brace itself should be highlighted using either white paint or tape (the same goes for a French brace). This will ensure that actors and staff in transit across the stage will not trip over the offending brace, making the set shake or damaging themselves. All potential danger spots should be carefully marked by the stage management – you only know if you've forgotten to mark something when it is too late. The nose of each tread on a set of get-off steps should be marked in white, as should the handrail. It is also useful to mark the off-stage edge of any legs or offstage wing flats to ensure that no one walks into them.

It can be very helpful to mark an entrance with the most extreme line of sight on the floor, to ensure that an actor does not find himself looking straight at a member of the audience prior to his entrance.

Provision should be made for a working light for each prop table and working lights for any corridor areas backstage. If there is a quick change area, lighting provision must also be made for these. All such lights are usually heavily coloured with blue but it is important that you check none of them are allowed to spill onto the stage at a point when total darkness is required. The supply and positioning of these backstage working lights must be negotiated with the Electrics department.

It will show a deal of foresight if you are able to provide a mirror above one of the stage left and stage right prop tables. It can also make backstage infinitely more comfortable for all concerned if water is provided stage left and stage right, but never serve water in glass receptacles, for this would create an unnecessary danger.

All cables emanating from dip traps in the floor should be stuck down with carpet tape. The use of wool-based carpet runners to cover these cables will also result in a quieter backstage area.

Where possible, provision should be made for cue lights on entrances, even if they have not been requested. It so often happens that actors get on stage and it suddenly strikes them that they cannot see through the set to take their cue (it should have struck the stage management weeks beforehand). Doors are always a problem onstage for the ball catches are often too strong and need adjustment. The doors themselves have a tendency not to remain where they are positioned if they are set ajar or fully open. There are two possible answers to this problem. The first involves putting a screw-eye in the back of the door with a corresponding screw-eye in the face of the masking flat offstage. A length of cord is attached to the screw-eye on the door and threaded downwards through the screw-eye on the masking flat. On the end of this cord a weight is hung that counterbalances the movement of the door so that it will remain static wherever it is positioned, using the pull of the rake.

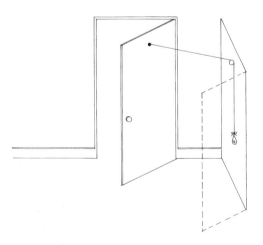

8.2 Door counterweight

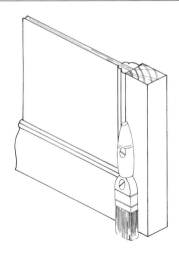

8.3 *Door friction brush*

An alternative to this, which can be equally as effective and yet more discreet, is to screw an inch (25mm) wide fresh paint brush to the offstage bottom edge of the door. The bristle creates a friction on the floor that is both silent and smooth, yet it effectively retains the door in whatever position it is left.

All locks, bolts and keys should not be practical – that is they should not in any way lock or secure the door or window. All doors for use on stage should be fitted with an adjustable ball catch only.

SCENE CHANGES

Scene changes are akin to a military operation – a comparison which is indicative of the forward planning that is required to ensure a smooth operation. The days of total set change for each new act, with people rushing around changing large pieces of scenery are, I am delighted to say, passing. With the increased use of motorized trucks bringing completed sets on from the wings, bridge lifts that raise sets from under the stage, revolving turntables (revolves) that spin on a new scene and

increased flying facilities, the job is getting easier. Nevertheless, there is still a strong need for good scene change organization.

You must first establish the job that has to be done by placing side by side the pre-set plan for the act to come and the final layout of scenery and props for the last act. The fundamental requirements of the scene changes should have been analyzed in the very early stages of production when the stage manager, director and designer all sat down with the production manager to discuss how they would be carried out. If a change is to be labour intensive it will have a major impact on the budget which, if it is to be a long run, will influence the overall cost-effectiveness of the play. If there is to be a large amount of flying that must all take place at once this will also increase the number of staff. Likewise, if a piece of scenery is to be made light enough to be a one-man lift the expense of building it to a specialist brief will add to costs.

Provision must be made for the props and scenery coming off the stage as much as for those going on. A prop table should be allocated to receive props and it must be positioned next to the table from which the props are to be collected. Each trip onto the stage must not be wasted and every move made while on stage must be used to maximum advantage. Routes across the stage should be worked out on a ground plan to ensure that those involved do not bump into one another. It can be more effective to put two people on a piece of scenery even if it could be carried by one if this means that it will travel off stage and on stage more accurately, more quickly and more quietly. The goals of a good scene change are:

Accuracy
Speed
Silence

Accuracy is obviously of prime importance – if the prop or piece of scenery is not where it should be then it will not be fulfilling its role and might as well not be there. 'More speed, less haste' is a maxim which could (and should) be applied to every scene change. And while the change is in process, the stage management and crew will rarely be seen and definitely not heard.

If there is to be a total set change, the tabs may be brought in and the worker lights switched on while in the auditorium the audience listens to music which is theatrically appropriate and covers any noise made during the change. In a theatre in the round, however, the job becomes a little more tricky, for the whole change must be done in sight of the audience. Whether in an interval or indeed during the play any change must be skilfully choreographed.

With scenery the use of small and large trucks and linking flattage can be

THE BUS AND TRUCK THEATRE COMPANY

'JOURNEY'S END'

RUNNING PLOT

DURING 'HALF'		
Check damp sand in ashtrays and check positioning of fire extinguishers.		
DURING 'BEGINNERS':	7.25 pm	CS
Light on-stage candles (remain in attendance until acting company present)		
ON 'GO' FROM DSM: (As curtain rises)		
Wet Lieutenant Osborne's footwear	7.30 pm	SL
ON CALL FROM DSM (gap approx. 8 minutes):	7.38 pm	
Prepare cutlets		
ON MANSON'S EXIT:	P.7	SL
Collect items he has cleared from table. (Bottles, cups, papers)		
PRIOR TO RALEIGH'S ENTRANCE:	P.8	SL
Wet Broughton's and Raleigh's footwear		
PRIOR TO STANHOPE'S ENTRANCE:		
Wet his footwear	P.14	SR
MANSON'S SECOND ENTRANCE:	P.15	SL
Hand Manson two plates of soup and bottle of whisky.		
MANSON'S 3RD ENTRANCE:	P.15	SL
Hand Manson two plates of soup.		
PRIOR TO SOLDIER'S ENTRANCE:	P.16	SR
Wet his footwear.		
MANSON'S 4TH ENTRANCE:	P.17	SL
Hand Manson pan with cutlets and 4 knives and 4 forks.		
ON MANSON'S EXIT:	P.18	SL
Hand Manson tray of coffee.		

8.4 Running plot

extremely effective, as relatively complex set dressing can remain attached to the trucks. All of these considerations should be planned out well in advance with the designer during the pre-production period.

What happens to props in a scene change must also be well thought through. The papers positioned on a desk can all be previously stuck together and stuck to the knee-hole of the desk out of sight, so they don't actually leave the stage. The game of patience neatly laid out on the table can be threaded together on a line of fine cat gut so that they can be picked up with one hand. The tray of drinks that is carried on in the change will have all but the one bottle actually used stuck to the tray. There is always an answer to any problem if you can give it a little thought.

Again, it must be emphasized that accuracy is your main aim, and it should not be sacrificed for speed. The use of marks for furniture during light changes will ensure correct positioning; the use of luminous marks for blackout changes is almost essential. Closing your eyes before a blackout change is an old but effective device that greatly improves your vision in the dark (if you then remember to open your eyes).

Marks for performance should be visible but not become a principal part of the floor design. The upstage edge/legs of a piece of furniture should be marked with a ½ x ½ inch (12.5 mm) square of marking tape, not with distracting large PVC crosses.

All scene changes will be part of an overall 'running plot' that has been developed through rehearsal. A running plot indicates which actor will need assistance, what sound effect will occur, the props in use and all the scenic jobs that have to be done throughout the performance. For example, a tray of drinks is collected from an actor as he comes off a brightly lit stage to a dark wing and is temporarily blind. The actor would put the tray down himself if he could see the prop table. These sort of details make the performance work (even down to reminding the forgetful actor to take props with him). The running plot should list the script page, the action to be taken and on what side of the stage, and say which ASM will fulfil the task (see fig. 8:4). If possible each active member of the stage crew and all the stage management should be given their own running plots.

9. On the Book

PROMPTING

Up to this point in the production process the DSM has been in rehearsal, working on the prompt book. During the lighting and sound rehearsal the DSM is found in the stalls, having direct contact with the director, designer and lighting designer in order to confirm the sequence, duration and position of cues in the text. When this task is complete the DSM relocates to the pre-arranged prompt corner, which is usually located downstage left, just off stage – if it is situated in a similar position stage right it is referred to as the 'bastard prompt'! The position of the prompt corner should allow a good view of the stage and the action that will take place and it can be improved, though crudely, by a mirror on the upstage side of the proscenium arch. Nowadays it is very often possible to have a television monitor in front of the DSM showing a central view of the stage. In some conventional theatres it may be possible to reposition the prompt corner in a stage box in the auditorium although this will mean that the communication systems on which the DSM relies has to be repositioned. In a studio theatre, the DSM may be situated behind glass so that the business of running the show does not infringe on the play itself. On occasions such as this a separate prompt would be positioned in the audience as an insurance policy against drying actors. Under normal circumstances, however, it will be the DSM who provides a prompt.

Prompting in performance is a difficult job at the best of times but it does rely primarily on the professional spontaneity of the prompter (DSM). He/she will have nursed the actors through the rehearsal process and will therefore have both an intimate knowledge of the text and the actors' delivery. Pauses and moves will be marked into the prompt script but a knowledge of a particular actor's delivery will be key to the question of whether or not to prompt. This is the tricky decision that falls to all prompters. The very idea that someone can prompt effectively who does not have an intimate knowledge of the play and its players is simply ridiculous.

When an actor dries it is usually obvious to those in the know except, curiously, it is very often not apparent to the actors themselves. The DSM/prompt may well be found prompting without consciously thinking that is what is about to happen.

A prompt should be loud, well articulated and contain a sufficiently large piece of the text as to allow the actor in question to identify it. The prompt should always endeavour to 'point' the prompt at the actor for it has been known for the cast to reply 'Yes, darling we know the line but who says it?' If there is a vocal warm-up for the cast it can benefit the DSM to participate in this so the actors know that the prompter is also in control of his/her voice and can use it when necessary.

A prompter who jumps in too quickly can destroy a performance, but a slow prompt in answer to a request for one from the stage can have an equally destructive effect. A DSM has to keep an eye on the text and on the actors, in similar measure.

CUEING

Communication is the key to stage management, and is nowhere more important than in dress rehearsal and performance. Cues must be given to those onstage, and also lighting, and sound technicians and fly crew. Intercoms are currently used for most forms of communication, but these must be used in a disciplined way, avoiding chatter and making sure that everyone completely understands the information passed on. Prior to a cue being actioned it is given a standby that alerts the operator to the impending cue. This is usually given

MOVES	CALLS
1. EVANS ENT USR X DSR	WORKERS OUT + BLACKOUT CHECK
2. EVANS X CS	HALF HOUR CALL – 35 MINS
3. EVANS X USL HATCH ENT DSL	QUARTER HOUR CALL – 20 MINS
	FIVE MINS CALL – 10 MINS
	BEGINNERS CALL : MR HALL MR JOHNSON MR HENSHAW STAGE MANAGEMENT
	3 MINUTE BELL 2 MINUTE BELL 1 MINUTE BELL
	FOH CLEARANCE S/B BEGINNERS ON STAGE
	CALL: CURTAIN UP ACT ONE S/B CREW FOR SCENE CHANGE MISS MARTINDALE MISS WINN

9.1 Prompt copy

approximately one to two minutes before the cue, with the words 'standby electrics cue 12' and it should be verbally acknowledged by the operator. If the following cue is very close to cue 12 then the standby is expanded to include cue 13. This is then followed through with 'electrics cue 12 GO'. The timing of the GO for any cue must of course relate to the onstage action but it will also be dictated by the speed with which an operation can

be carried out and when that operation will have an effect on the action of the performance. This can be referred to as 'anticipating a cue' and for a cue to be completely effective it must happen in pace with the performers. If there is to be a DBO (dead blackout) at the end of a comic scene, it is imperative that the cue is given on the right beat to ensure that the blackout is achieved at just the right comic moment. If the cue is given *at the*

CUES

PRESET

LX Q1 (PRESET + HOUSELIGHTS)

SOUND Q1 (HOUSE MUSIC)

ON S/B OF BEGINNERS:

S/B LXQ2,3,4

S/B SOUND Q2,3,4

ON CLEARANCE FROM SM:

SOUND Q2 GO (10 SEC FADE ↑ 4 SEC FADE ↓)

10 SEC | GAP
↓

LX Q2 GO (HOUSE OUT 8 SEC)

6 SEC | GAP
↓

LX Q3 GO (FLASH ON CYC)

4 SEC | GAP
↓

LX Q4 GO (BUILD STAGE)

10 SEC | GAP
↓

S.L WING GO (WILLY)

5 SEC | GAP
↓

SOUND Q3 GO (10 SEC FADE ↓)

SOUND Q4 GO (THUNDER)

SCENE ONE

Beach.

Empty stage. Darkness and thunder. Wind roars, whines, crashes and screams over the water. Masses of water swell up, rattle and churn, and crash back into the sea. Gravel and sand grind slowly. The earth trembles.

WILLY. Help. Aaahhh – (*The sound is drowned by water.*) Help. Colin. Shout. Oh, god, make him shout.

The tempest grows louder.

WILLY. Help – (*The sound is drowned by water again.*)

A drunken man comes on singing.

① EVENS. I don't know why – I sing'ss song – 'Ss day'ss short – an' ss—
WILLY. Help. Help.
EVENS. Wha'?
WILLY. Here. In the water. A man's in the water.

Thunder.

② EVENS. 'Ss too late f'ss thass. 'Ss sea 'sl finish all'ss thass. Have'ss drink. Lil'ss drink. Here'ss, take'ss bottle . . .
WILLY. Help me. Our boat turned over. I can't find him.
EVENS. I sing 'ss song – 'Ss day'ss short – an'ss —
WILLY. You bastard. Colin. Colin.
EVENS. Wah'? I don' know why'ss – 'Ssing'ss song – 'Ss some'ss in'ss wasser? ③

The storm is worse. Thunder. The wind screams. HATCH, *a middle-aged man, comes on with a torch.*

HATCH. What are you up to?

moment it will be activated too late and the effect will be lost.

It is therefore the job of the DSM to anticipate the action onstage to allow sufficient time for the operation of the cue.

If the DSM is to do this, there has to be a continuity in performance, which means the actors should perform the play as directed. If video is being used, the pre-roll time can be as long as five seconds and to ensure the playback comes at the right point requires very precise anticipation.

Methods of communication can vary from a piece of string attached to the electrician's leg, 'pull once for standby and twice for go' or cue lights.

Cue lights are the most universal form of cue communication, giving a red light for a standby and a green for GO. The lights show in front of both the DSM and the person being cued, and are switched from the DSM's control board. Occasionally there may be a red reply button at the operator's end which allows the operator

MOVES	CALLS
1. WILLY ENT SL XCS	
2. HATCH EXITS SR	
3. WILLY EXITS USL.	

9.2 Prompt copy

to acknowledge the standby by flashing the red light to say 'I am standing by'.

If a cue is given by the DSM it must be acted on. Nor is it acceptable for the lighting operator to anticipate a cue and go before the cue is given. The prompt script represents the central focus for all technical departments. Each department has cue sheets, from which they will act on a cue given from one source, the DSM. On some occasions cues may be taken by operators on a visual cue from the action. This will be given a standby by the DSM and carefully monitored when operated.

The place from which tannoy announcements can be made both to the dressing rooms and sometimes FOH is usually found in the prompt corner. Integrated in this system will also be the show relay switch that pipes the onstage action into the dressing rooms, green room and backstage area. Close to, if not in the prompt corner will also be found the following:

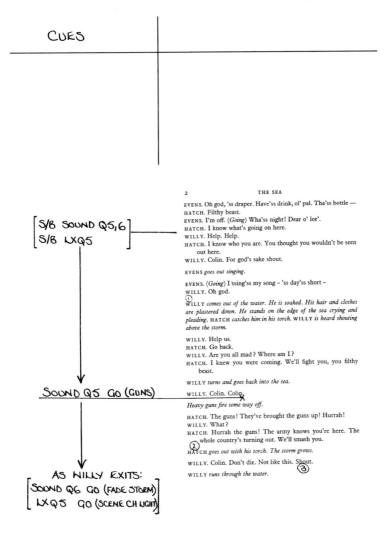

CUES

S/B SOUND Q5,6
S/B LXQ5

SOUND Q5 GO (GUNS)

AS WILLY EXITS:
SOUND Q6 GO (FADE STORM)
LXQ5 GO (SCENE CH LIGHT)

2   THE SEA

EVENS. Oh god, 'ss draper. Have'ss drink, ol' pal. Tha'ss bottle —
HATCH. Filthy beast.
EVENS. I'm off. (*Going*) Wha'ss night! Dear o' lor'.
HATCH. I know what's going on here.
WILLY. Help. Help.
HATCH. I know who you are. You thought you wouldn't be seen
    out here.
WILLY. Colin. For god's sake shout.

EVENS *goes out singing.*

EVENS. (*Going*) I 'ssing'ss my song – 'ss day'ss short –
WILLY. Oh god.
WILLY *comes out of the water. He is soaked. His hair and clothes
are plastered down. He stands on the edge of the sea crying and
pleading.* HATCH *catches him in his torch.* WILLY *is heard shouting
above the storm.*

WILLY. Help us.
HATCH. Go back.
WILLY. Are you all mad? Where am I?
HATCH. I knew you were coming. We'll fight you, you filthy
    beast.

WILLY *turns and goes back into the sea.*

WILLY. Colin. Colin.
Heavy guns fire some way off.
HATCH. The guns! They've brought the guns up! Hurrah!
WILLY. What?
HATCH. Hurrah! the guns! The army knows you're here. The
    whole country's turning out. We'll smash you.
HATCH *goes out with his torch. The storm grows.*
WILLY. Colin. Don't die. Not like this. Shout.
WILLY *runs through the water.*

Working light switches
Effect activation switches
Clock (from which the show is run)
Reading lights
Release for the safety curtain

The DSM should be familiar with all these elements well before the technical rehearsal starts.

The preceding pages from a fictitious performance of *The Sea* by Edward Bond show the way that a prompt script is structured (see figs. 9.1 and 9.2). There is no tabs cue in the opening sequence as the audience walked in to see the stage set for the first scene. Note how there is an indication between the cues to state the gap between them. This can also be used to give a visual reference for a cue if it is an action rather than a word. Against each cue a timing should be marked, indicating the duration of the cue.

10. Production Rehearsals

STOPPING DRESS REHEARSAL

The stopping dress rehearsal is given a number of names in the industry: the tech, the technical rehearsal or the stagger through. The latter term conjures a vision of an event that is on its last legs and quite uncontrolled. This should certainly not be the case, for at this stage in the production process you cannot afford to allow anything to get out of hand.

The stopping dress is there to iron out the remaining practical issues relating to a production. The rehearsal period has given ample opportunity to examine interpretation and for the purposes of this particular rehearsal these aspects must be put to one side. Its function is to come to terms with the practical aspects of the production; lighting and sound cues, entrances and exits and, of course, scene and costume changes, which to this point you have not been able to rehearse. The smooth running of this event will in large part, depend on the stage management team having worked effectively throughout the production process.

You have implemented early problem analysis, which has ensured that the practical staging problems have been solved well in advance and all those involved are *aware* of the solution. If this has involved specific pieces of action with specific props, the props have been found and their use has been fully rehearsed. Your painstakingly detailed rehearsal notes have been distributed and followed through.

Personal props off and onstage and setting of stage props will already have been agreed.

At the stopping dress rehearsal the cast will, for the first time, be confronted with the real doors and windows – up to now these have been but lines on the floor of the rehearsal room. No matter how exact the mark-out in rehearsal has been, the cast will always initially be slightly shocked; things always seem different in three dimensions! At this point, however, the cast will be grateful that you have persisted in reminding them of the hinged direction of doors, the sightlines on entrances and all practical rehearsal details.

To soften the blow, it is often useful to have a walk around the set with the cast prior to the start of the stopping dress rehearsal. You can then take them round the stage in full light and explain the positioning of the prop tables, lights, mirrors and jars of water backstage and reaffirm the positioning of items on the stage. The cast will be able to try the catches on the doors and get their door acting right, whilst checking the relationship of pieces of furniture and hand props. Have a props person and a carpenter close to hand at this stage. This will allow the door catches to be adjusted there and then while also being able to fine tune the prop setting. Allowing the cast this try out time, if not allowed to get out of hand, can very often take time off the overall running time of the stopping dress. And in these final stages of production, time is the adversary of all.

As its name would infer 'stopping' is an integral part of a stopping dress rehearsal. The rehearsal itself should contain all the elements that have been compiled to stage the play: sound, light, effects, scenery, props, costume.

The sound content such as background effects and special effects will probably be new to the actors but buzzers and bells will have been used in the rehearsal process. The lighting will, of course, be new and be of equal concern to the actor as the costume and props. It has been known for an actor to stop mid-flow in a stopping dress and ask 'Can I be seen in this light?' The correct directorial response, to my mind, should be 'Yes – and on please' and not 'Oh, we've been wondering about that...' (The director could easily have the lighting adjusted as the scene continues by liaising with the lighting designer at the production desk in the stalls.)

The scenery and props should not represent a problem to the cast as the props have been in previous rehearsals and they have had an opportunity to walk the stage prior to this rehearsal. The costumes should also have been sorted out in the dress parade and any quick changes should have been rehearsed and timed separately beforehand.

If the rehearsal is ill-prepared and therefore time-consuming tempers will fray and patience will wear thin; time is so important right now and all those present are aware of it. It can be effective if the director and stage manager get together to agree the working parameters of the rehearsal, i.e., who calls for a stop in the action, what action will be taken at that moment and how the rehearsal will be resumed. The basic scheme having been established, it should be conveyed to the company in clear terms prior to starting.

At this point the director may request a voice of God microphone to address those on stage (when required) during the rehearsal. This request should be examined carefully, for a microphone in the hands of an anxious director can be a retrogressive step. During this rehearsal, more than any other time in the production process, the stage manager is caught up in the anxiety of others and a strong managerial hand is required on the tiller. If the action has to be stopped for one reason or another, the stage manager should be there onstage to sort it out, immediately if not sooner, armed with a pen and paper to write notes for reference and to reassure all concerned that the problem is being committed to paper. The stage manager should not hide behind the scenery but should be there where the problem is, and available at the front of the stage to talk to the director in the stalls. If the problem relates to a prop the ASM/prop master responsible should be onstage with a paper and pencil too. It is essential that the moment the rehearsal stops the problem is identified, for once it is identified you can then be certain when it has been solved. Many a delay has been caused by those involved asking why they have stopped and not getting an answer. They are then reluctant to start again without solving the original problem so they must know what the problem was in the first place.

Managing those more tricky moments when 'all those around you are losing their heads and blaming it on you' is difficult. It is inevitable that there are occasions when this might happen and clear thinking at this point is essential. When the levels of anxiety are running high, it is human nature to look for an outlet and you may be it. You must not take the issues personally and you must not lose your temper or you will show that you have lost control of the situation. You

Stopping Dress Rehearsal Checklist

- Check that all the props are set on and offstage
- Check with all departments that they are set for the elected start time: wardrobe, sound, lighting, flys
- Check everything is safe: no unmarked steps, stray colour frames, hidden stage braces, curling carpet, hanging cables. A clean theatre is a safe and quiet theatre
- Check the tannoy is on and working
- Walk the set to do a final check of doors, windows and see that furniture is on its marks
- Call the dressing rooms with the half, quarter and five minute calls but do not call the actors at beginners' until you know that you are ready to start. If there is to be photography during the rehearsal, at the quarter call the dressing rooms with "May I remind members of the company, photos will be taken during the stopping dress rehearsal.' (NB: this means that all props, set, wigs and costumes must be as performance – if not, you must inform the director and photographers of the problem.)
- Check all cue lights, telephone bells, buzzers etc.
- Make sure you have a list of beginners for the start of each act and scene
- Ensure the 'Quiet, please' notices are up in the relevant surrounding corridors
- Check the blackout to make sure all worker lights are out
- Take a note of the curtain calls: order of entrances, order in the line-up, number of bows, tabs and blackout and post on board immediately
- Check availability of refreshments for the duration of rehearsal
- Check wardrobes can supply smocks for actors during a refreshment break to ensure that they do not mark their costumes
- Check with wardrobe, sound, props and DSM as to how long the reset will take at the end of the stopping dress so that you can inform the production manager, who will allow for accurate scheduling in the evening or days ahead
- Have a pre-cut board of coloured marking tape to mark furniture; there may well be changes made in the position of the furniture throughout this rehearsal

must identify the real problem and this is not as easy as it might first appear because in most cases people come to you with the reactions and results of a problem and not the problem itself. You must therefore look past the reactions and results and focus on the root. As the saying goes 'When you are up to your armpits in alligators it is hard to remember that your first job was to drain the swamp.' The lesson in this is to focus on the main objective and delegate where possible to those closer to the heart of the issue. Don't be drawn into the thick of it otherwise you will not be in a position to manage all the other areas that need attention.

When there is a pause in the action the person on the book should immediately locate the point in the text from which the actors are to pick up the text. This enables the stage manager to push the proceedings forward by asking the actors to go from 'X when you are ready', having been fed the information by the person on the book.

When going back on an actor's cue, it is essential that all those involved know exactly what is happening and where (when the problem is solved) it is intended that the action starts again. Lighting may have to reset a cue, as may sound. The DSM must liaise with the technical department to ensure that if they have had to go back on a cue that reset is complete, or if a change has to be made that change is logged. The DSM must also ensure that enough time is given to write in a cue change so the department is not just guessing it when they next operate the cue in question. This equally applies to the

---

Breaks Checklist

- Tell HODs ahead of time of your intention to stop. This allows them to plan the use of the time and break some of their staff early

- Announce over the tannoy and to the company onstage the length of the break and the time when the rehearsal will start again. If costume changes are involved the cast must be informed of which costume to be in for the start of rehearsal

- Give a call to your stage staff

- Switch off the dressing room tannoy – many overheard conversations have destroyed the unsuspecting listener

- Switch off the lights if not needed

- At five and three minutes before the starting time, call the beginners needed to restart the rehearsal and check that lighting and sound are ready to start again

DSM: it is extremely important that he/she does not change the content of any of the cueing sequences or delete anything which should not be deleted. Pencilled notes in the margin are not enough – each change must be carefully and accurately noted. Props may have to be reset to allow the actors to go back. If you have cause to stop while a costume change is happening it often benefits all to press those on stage to continue until the change is complete, particularly if it is a complex change. If however, you absolutely have to stop at that point you must stop the change. It is essential that the stage manager remains in control of the situation, allowing actors to proceed only when all the other departments are ready to continue.

Again, it is worth emphasising that a little time spent now ensuring that alterations in the staging of the play are recorded properly will ensure that changes made at this point will be implemented at future performances. The stage manager must not allow himself to be pressurized by conflicting demands, and should make sure that enough time is given to solve the problem and record the answer. The DSM will be responsible for seeing that all the technical departments are resetting and recording information in response to stage activity. The stage manager should also be able to evaluate whether actors need to repeat their actions in full in order to provide the cueing point for an effect. As a rule of thumb, it is normally of benefit to the actor, technician and overall production to repeat the stage action in full so as to give all concerned an understanding of the pace and content of that action.

If, by mismanagement, a stop is allowed to extend to shall we say, two minutes (which happens easily if you are not careful), and you stop thirty times, you have just added one hour to the whole rehearsal process. At this stage you have

the full company waiting for the result of a stop: sound, lights, stage management, wardrobe, stage crew and actors in hot or cold costumes. It is a waste of money and goodwill to have all these people hanging around waiting to solve a problem that could have been solved in rehearsal or on paper two weeks earlier. About three to four times the running time of the play should be allowed for the stopping dress rehearsal, which is indicated on the schedule provided on page 77. You will, of course, have to provide a number of breaks for all concerned. It can be worth consulting with your HODs ahead of the time you intend to break. This can allow them to break some of their staff early so they can work on stage while everyone else is on a break. The 'breaks checklist' should help you to organize this (see page 109).

THE DRESS REHEARSALS

There is a lot to achieve in the intervening period between a stopping dress rehearsal and the dress rehearsal. Technical adjustments to lighting, sound and staging may have to be effected, to say nothing of the wardrobe turnround that will require wigs to be reset and costumes washed, pressed and laid out. The stage management during this time will need to ensure that the stage is scenically reset and the props are reset for the start of the performance. Meanwhile the DSM will be deeply engrossed in amending and tidying up the prompt copy. When doing this the DSM must be extremely careful not to change the content of any cueing sequences or delete that which should not be deleted. This is one of the reasons why it is so extremely important that the DSM takes time during the stopping dress rehearsal to make accurate changes to cueing sequences rather than pencilling notes in the margin.

The reset time should have been taken into account when the original production schedule was drawn up. If the technical rehearsal overruns then the pressure will be on to meet the deadline of the dress rehearsal. On occasion a compromise has to be made and the stage manager should be there to liaise between departments, director and cast. When the reset is complete and everyone has eaten (most important) the dress rehearsal can start.

Dress rehearsals must be treated as a real performance; no member of the company should be allowed FOH and all the technical aspects of this performance should be as they will be for the first night. Calls to the company should be made as if for a performance, giving a half-hour call thirty-five minutes before the start of the performance. On the 'half' the stage management should ensure that all the cast and crew are present, for though it will not happen at this rehearsal it is customary to open the doors of the auditorium thirty minutes before announcing the start of the play. In most theatres the cast will sign in at the stage door, if not report to the prompt corner. During a dress rehearsal the company should not have left the building so it may be advisable to send round a member of the stage management to ensure that they have not relocated to the pub round the corner. When dealing with an orchestra it would be advisable at this point to look in the pub first and the band room second. With some forethought the management of the King's Theatre (Edinburgh) have installed a bell in the pub next door. This ensures the presence of the orchestra in the pit as well as the public in their seats.

A tour round the dressing rooms, checking the cast, can also be combined with issuing personal props where

Dress Rehearsal Checklist

FIRST DRESS REHEARSAL

- Ensure the 'Quiet, please' notices are up in the surrounding corridors
- Check with catering manager as to availability of coffee for the interval
- Check that all staff are wearing the correct footwear and clothes
- Check all timing and notes for show report
- Check that you have a room allocated for notes the next day and that notes are put up on the call board. Also allocate a member of stage management to go to the note session

SECOND DRESS REHEARSAL

- Times to FOH manager
- Ensure the "Quiet, please' notices are up in the surrounding corridors
- NB: No one is allowed FOH during a performance. Full FOH blackout

appropriate. In a normal performance situation you will check dressing rooms and facilities while discussing the events of the day and the possible size of the evening's audience with the cast. On the occasion of a dress rehearsal, however, the cast will not be in the mood for tittle tattle and you will no doubt have a lot of other things to do. It's a good idea to have a word with the director prior to the dress rehearsal to discuss the time and place of the inevitable 'notes' session that will be called after the rehearsal, which is for the benefit of all involved in the production. It can, however, be advantageous to agree that technical notes are given separately so as not to bore the pants off either the production staff or the cast.

The technical notes that the director gives will relate to the cueing of effects, the nature of those effects, properties and the scenic elements. At this stage the director will be tightening down on the detail of the production and his comments should not be taken as a personal criticism. There may be a hundred and one technical reasons for the miscueing of an effect or the misplacing of a prop. I believe it is fair to say that most directors do not wish to hear the story of why something went wrong, they merely wish to be told that you know why it happened and be assured that his specification will be followed in the future.

The notes sessions themselves can take place in the stalls of the theatre. Alternatively, they can take place in the green room or rehearsal room of the theatre. The DSM should be present for both the technical and actors' notes, for the DSM must have a complete understanding of the actors' performances if he/she is to fulfil the role.

11. First Night

And so to the first night, where the tensions of the past weeks are washed away in the flow of adrenalin, and everyone is filled with relief that the day has come. There will be tight smiles, 'Good Luck' cards and you will wonder what all the fuss was about when the curtain falls.

The stage management will be required to conjure vases for flowers from nowhere and Blu-tack for cards from everywhere. The props have been reset and checked, the odd actor has popped down to prowl the set one more time (muttering phrases that are only just discernible as his lines) and all is ready.

The director is found in the dressing rooms, still giving last minute notes to a listening but far-away actor and has to be propelled to the bar. The dressers flit from room to room attending to those last minute details that have to be urged upon some actors and with others quashed.

The half-hour call given, the stage manager now confident that all his/her actors and crew are assembled, the DSM is sent with the personal props for a quick circuit of the dressing rooms and an ASM is left on stage to keep a watchful eye. The SM steps through the pass door into the brightly lit auditorium to meet, as arranged, the FOH manager. Both parties survey the auditorium for stray workers left on – the stage manager in fact knows that the whole theatre was taken to black-out and the lighting states built up from the Lx board in the preset and systems check, but must show willing. Having

checked there is no sign of any production detritus that the cleaners have missed and with the ushers in place, it is jointly agreed that the auditorium is ready to open, for it is now 7 o'clock.

You are at that moment standing on the FOH manager's territory but the liaison between the stage manager and the FOH manager is something to be emphasised. You will both be able to help each other in so many ways, and it has to be worth making the very best of this relationship.

The stage manager returns to the backstage area via the FOH (collecting programmes for the company if they have not been circulated before) in time to hear the quarter call by the DSM from the prompt corner. From this point onwards it is very, very unlikely that the DSM will leave the prompt corner until the interval. After the curtain has risen the DSM is pledged on pain of death to remain alert in the prompt corner. While seated, the DSM will implement a check to confirm that all the crew are now in place for the start of the performance, known as a 'cans check' if a ring intercom system is used as a means of communication. The stage manager should confirm with the director whether or not he wishes to rehearse the next day, and, if so, he will post the understudy call sheet on the noticeboard for the following day. (If the stage manager were a West End company manager it would be his responsibility to both call and take the rehearsal.)

At the five minute call the stage manager will go directly to the stage to ensure all is well. At the 'beginners' call the relevant members of the company will start to arrive on stage and the SM can check off those present and their starting positions against the beginners' list for Act One. While the stage manager checks the company, the DSM will give the final dressing room call, 'beginners on stage' which will start the sequence of the three announcements and bells to FOH, given by the DSM.

Having got all the actors in place the SM will give the set one last check, looking at the setting of the doors and windows while waiting for FOH clearance. This can take the form of the FOH manager in person arriving backstage or an internal phone call to say that all is ready FOH. From this call the SM will switch off the workers and ask the DSM to 'Go'. Having already put the crew on standby, the 'go' can be rapidly implemented and the stopwatch is now started for the timing of the performance.

On curtain up, the DSM will announce 'Curtain up, Act One' to the backstage area and the show relay will be switched on. Calls will also be given to the backstage area to summon members of the company to the stage for their entrance. These are courtesy calls but should be marked in the text and given at the same time each night, allowing enough time for the actors to assemble themselves and arrive at the stage level. Four minutes seems to be a reasonable minimum time to allow but it is very dependent on the distance that the actor has to travel from his dressing room. These calls are given in alphabetical order, ladies first, using the actors' real names (Ms Bond, Miss Jones, Mr Smith).

If there are understudies on, then the DSM in particular and all the stage management should be on the ball. The crew will also need calling for special effects, scene changes etc.

ALL OF THESE CALLS MUST BE INTEGRATED INTO THE RUNNING OF THE SHOW FROM AND INCLUDING THE STOPPING DRESS REHEARSAL.

The stage manager should endeavour to keep time as free as possible to allow an opportunity to view the performance from the auditorium (quality control) and to deal with any firefighting situation that may arise. It is imperative that the stage manager lets the rest of the stage management know where to find him/her when absent from the stage. The tannoy can easily be used to summon the SM when required on stage in the case of an emergency! However, due to financial and practical necessity, the stage manager often gets deeply involved in the running of the show. The SM's first obligation is to be on stage to manage the work of the staff and the actors in his or her charge.

Prior to the interval it is customary to ring the bar bell once, five minutes before the interval should begin. This, however, to my mind can only be done, if the bar bell in question is not audible in the auditorium. Otherwise, the stage manager should call FOH on the in-house telephone.

During the interval the company usually find themselves gathering round for coffee in the green room. Beware at this stage of being critical of performances for all those concerned will be extremely sensitive. Interval bells and beginners are called in exactly the same way as is used for the beginning of the performance. The stage manager will again continue the performance, having been given clearance from FOH.

The DSM will again immediately call the dressing rooms at the start of the new act: 'Curtain up, Act two'. As the end of the play approaches the DSM will call 'Full company stand by for curtain down, Act Two and curtain calls'. When the curtain falls on the last moment of the play there will be an immediate requirement for light backstage to ensure that the cast have an opportunity to regroup for the curtain calls. This light can either be an upstage preset courtesy of the lighting operator or a worker light. If a worker is to be used then the SM will ensure that it is switched off before the curtain rises on the curtain calls.

The pattern of the curtain calls will have been set at the end of the first dress rehearsal. The order, line up and formation will have been posted on the call board. When the set bows are complete, traditionally the curtain will fall, and before the tabs hit the deck the decision has to be made as to whether another curtain call will be taken. This is because it is impossible for the tab operator to turn a stop cleanly into a bounce – a bounce being when the tabs fleetingly touch the stage and immediately rise again. The decision to go for another curtain call is usually in the hands of the stage manager, who will stand beside the DSM and call 'Again' if another call is required or, 'No more' if he/she wishes the process to stop. This can sometimes be a very tricky decision.

When the cast have been given enough time to return to their dressing rooms, the DSM should announce, 'Thank you, ladies and gentlemen. May I remind members of the company that the next performance of . . . will be tomorrow night at 7.30. Thank you and goodnight'.

It is at this point that the DSM can announce the following day's rehearsal for understudies or possibly an exchange of notes session. Company announcements should, if at all possible, be kept to the end of the play.

The tannoy should always be switched off at the end of the evening and before notes.

Unfortunately, the stage management's jobs for the day have not yet finished. Valuable props should be locked away, personal props should be collected and the show report must be typed up. A show report, see fig. 11.1, should detail the times at which the curtain rose and fell for each act, and the duration of both acts and intervals to give a total running time for the show. The show report should also list in an objective way any large textual errors by the cast, miscues, prop damage, or indeed any extraordinary event.

It is only left for the stage manager to post the report internally to the director or by mail to the production company on the way to enjoying a well-earned drink with the rest of the company. The production is now in performance.

SHOW REPORT

PRODUCTION:- JACK AND THE BEANSTALK

DATE:- 24TH DECEMBER 1996

	UP	DOWN	PLAYING TIME	INTERVAL
ACT ONE	7.30	8.45	75 MINS	
INTERVAL	/	/	/	18 MINS
ACT TWO	9.03	10.10	67 MINS	
TOTALS			142 MINS	18 MINS
TOTAL SHOW RUNNING TIME			2 HRS 40 MINS	

REMARKS:

1. Mr Melmoth dried P.48 'That's one bean too many' but recovered with a prompt.

2. S.L. Truck winch sticking during first scene change; interval extended by 3 mins to allow inspection of guide track. Obstruction located and removed (boiled sweet presumably thrown from audience).

3. Four curtain calls were taken.

11.1 Show report

CURTAIN UP ROUTINE AND CALLS

The performance is to start at 7.30.
Check all the props and the set before the half.

6.55   1   CALL THE HALF:
             'Good evening, Ladies and Gentlemen.
             This is your half-hour call. Half an hour, please.'

        2   *All cast to report to the SM in the prompt corner (or sign in at the stage door).*

        3   *Re-check prop settings, practical doors etc.*

        4   *Personal props issued.*

        5   *Check auditorium is clear.*

        6   *Take all of the stage and auditorium to blackout and build lighting needed for performance.*

7.00   ONE LONG BELL TO FOH *(To open the house)*

7.10   CALL THE QUARTER:
        'Ladies and Gentlemen, this is your fifteen minute call. Fifteen minutes, please.'

7.20   CALL THE FIVE MINUTE CALL:
        'Ladies and Gentlemen, this is your five minute call. Five minutes please.'

7.25   CALL BEGINNERS ACT ONE:
        'Beginners Act One please. Miss Brown, Miss Fields, Mr Allsopp, Mr Smith:
        Then repeat

7.27   THREE BELLS TO FOH FOLLOWED BY:
        'Ladies and Gentlemen, will you please take your seats as the performance will begin in three minutes.'
        Then repeat

7.28   TWO BELLS TO FOH FOLLOWED BY:
        'Ladies and Gentlemen, will you please take your seats as the performance will begin in two minutes.'
        Then repeat

7.29   ONE BELL TO FOH FOLLOWED BY:
        'Ladies and Gentlemen, will you please take your seats as the performance is about to begin.'
        Then repeat

7.30   THE STAGE MANAGER WAITS FOR GO FROM FOH MANAGER
        When the go is given by the FOH Manager the SM returns to the stage and checks

        1   *All the beginners are in place and asks them to 'Stand by please'.*

2   *The tabs (operator) and any other crew needed at the start of the play are in position.*

3   *The setting of the doors on the set and lighting pre-set.*
When satisfied the SM will give the go to the DSM.

Call   ON CURTAIN UP, CALL DRESSING ROOMS
'Curtain up, Act One'.

Bells   FIVE MINUTES TO INTERVAL AND END OF PLAY: ONE BELL FOH.

Call   DURING INTERVAL BEGINNERS ACT TWO ARE CALLED AS ABOVE AND FOH BELLS ARE RUNG AT 3, 2, AND 1 MINUTE INTERVALS, GIVING THE FOH CALLS USING THE WORDING:
'Ladies and Gentlemen, will you please take your seats as the performance will resume in (3 mins)' and repeat.

SM TAKE GO FROM FOH MANAGER FOLLOWING THE SAME ROUTINE AS FOR ACT ONE.

Call   ON CURTAIN UP CALL DRESSING ROOMS
'Curtain up Act Two'.

Call   BEFORE THE END OF THE PLAY CALL TO THE DRESSING ROOMS:
'Fully Company standby for curtain down Act Two and curtain calls'.
And repeat

Call   AT THE END OF THE PLAY, *ONCE THE CAST HAVE RETURNED TO THEIR DRESSING ROOMS*, CALL TO THE DRESSING ROOMS:
'Ladies and Gentlemen, may I remind members of the company that the next performance of . . . will be tomorrow night at 7.30.'
Then repeat

'Thank you and goodnight'.

NB   The tannoy calls are usually all given by the DSM (or the person on the book except in a studio theatre).

The tannoy is not to be used for any private messages of good luck to the company.

Company announcements should, if possible, be kept to the end of the play. If this is not possible then the information should be delivered personally to each dressing room at the half and the quarter calls.

Switch off the tannoy at the end of the evening before notes.

Appendices

Appendix 1   Fire

Fire is potentially a major hazard in the theatre and all aspects of the fire regulations covering performance venues should be adhered to. Every theatre has sand-filled ashtrays at the doors that lead on to the stage. These should be kept clean of debris at all times. The 'no smoking' rule on stage (but for those in performance) must be kept. Fire extinguishers are not, as most people who work in the theatre seem to think, brightly coloured door stops for fire doors. Both are there to save lives in the event of a potential disaster. And fire doors have closers on them because they are meant to stay shut.

Electrical equipment must have close to hand a CO_2 extinguisher and not a water-filled appliance, for obvious reasons. The water and sand buckets often found in theatres are not waste bins and should be kept free from debris. The theatre as a whole must remain clear of rubbish and excess equipment that may block escape routes. Cables must be secured to the floor and where possible covered. This can be done using a wool based carpet that will also contribute to making the wings quieter. Ashtrays must be provided with damp sand inside them for those smoking as part of the performance, both on and offstage. The moment anyone enters the wings from the stage with a lit cigarette it must be put out immediately in an ashtray.

If a lit candle is to be included in a production the fire authorities must be informed and they will come to inspect how it will be used on stage. The basic rules are that the flame must be attended at all times with two crew members present when the flame is on stage, with extinguishers in their hands. The fire authorities may also require the scenery specification to be upgraded, and to be made of fire retardant timber (green stamp). Each area of the UK applies its regulations in different ways and the best route for any theatre is to ask the local fire department.

Most commercial theatres have a fireman in attendance during every performance and his responsibility will include the checking and unlocking of fire doors and routes to those doors. The fireman will also be responsible for the dropping and raising of the safety curtain in performances. By law the safety curtain (the iron) must be dropped in sight of the audience at every performance. This usually happens in the interval.

All drapes in the theatre must be fire-proof. This is tested by the visiting fireman at his inspection of the set and building that accompanies every new production and they do spring surprise visits on running shows. By applying a cigarette lighter to the edge of the cloth for thirty seconds the fireman determines if it will burn!

If it does not disappear in a sheet of flame you are OK. The masking in a theatre comes in three varieties: velour,

Bolton twill and serge. The serge has the advantage that as it is wool it is inherently fireproof. The others, along with curtains and drapes, have to be fireproofed. This involves immersing the cloth in a fireproofing solution that when dry is retained in the cloth and acts as a fire retardant. These solutions can crystallize on the fabric and eventually shake out. If any water is spilt on a piece of fireproofed fabric, white crystal rings will be formed that are the devil to get out.

To make up a simple flameproofing solution mix the ingredients below:

Borax   10oz/285g
Boracic   8oz/227g
Tepid Water   1 gallon/4½l
or
Boracic Acid   15oz/425g
Sodium Phosphate   10oz/285g
Tepid water   1 gallon/4½l

These are very crude mixtures and are for use cold. They will undoubtedly change the feel of the cloth. A dipped fabric should be hung up to dry and not wrung out. Other types of products are available on the market which can work effectively when sprayed on light fabrics and are water resistant when dry.

The safety curtain is made up of a sandwich of steel and asbestos. This curtain effectively acts as a draft excluder between the FOH and the backstage area, filling the whole of the proscenium arch, closing the hole in the fire wall. When released the iron rides down on air brakes which cause it to pause 18 inches/45 cm above the stage for a few seconds before finishing its descent. This pause is referred to as the dead man's gap, as it is there to allow any poor unfortunate that may be under the iron to be pulled away. When the iron is operated the operator should have a clear view of the iron line to be certain that there are no obstructions and herald it with a call of 'Iron coming in'.

The iron is usually installed next to a drencher system, a large pipe with holes in it above the iron. When released, mains pressure is applied to the pipe. The ensuing cascade of water coats the iron to cool it and assists in dowsing the flames.

Many theatres also have a lantern release that activates a set of spring-loaded panels at the top of the fly tower. When they open there is an upward draught causing the fire to be drawn up the fly tower and away from the rest of the building.

Every theatre has a 'fire word' which is usually in place of the word 'fire' so as to minimize the element of panic amongst the general public. This can mean that the fire takes on the name of a person i.e.: 'Mr Jet is in the green room' or 'Mr Sands is in the basement'. An evacuation procedure should be worked out in advance between the stage manager and FOH manager. The performance would be stopped by the tabs being dropped or the lights being faded onstage. The house lights would be faded up and usually the FOH manager would walk onstage to announce the evacuation of the audience while the SM evacuated the backstage area.

In the auditorium the ushers who have to be there by law would open the doors as the FOH manager announced:

'Owing to circumstances beyond our control, I must ask to you to leave the auditorium quietly by the nearest exit. Those with coats in the foyer please leave them where they are. There is no cause for alarm for the safety curtain will now be lowered.'

The last time I had to stop a show on the West End – it was due to yet another bomb scare – the company ended up giving a condensed performance of the last act of the play to the audience on the street!

Appendix 2 Copyright

What is copyright?:

The exclusive right to produce copies and control an original literary, musical or artistic work granted by law for a specified number of years. In Britain this is usually fifty years from the death of the author, composer etc. (or fifty years from the posthumous publication of a work). The typography of books published since September 1957 is also copyright from twenty-five years after publication, irrespective of whether the text or music is in copyright.

The infringement of copyright is something that every stage manager should beware of. In this day and age, given the ease with which we can photocopy material and cross-record on audio and video, we must be extremely careful that we do not take the copyright position of written and recorded material for granted.

Copyright is designed to protect the livelihood of the creators and producers of literary, dramatic, artistic and musical works. Photographs are normally the copyright of the person who commissioned them. Newspapers, however, are public property, with no restriction on reproduction rights. Making single copies of copyright material is acceptable for private study provided, as the law puts it, no more than a 'reasonable proportion' is copied.

Some years ago the Society of Authors and the Publishers Association stated that they would usually regard 'fair dealing' as: The use of a single extract of up to 400 words on a series of extracts (of which none exceeds 300 words) to a total of 800 words from a prose work, or extracts to a total of 40 lines from a poem, provided that this did not exceed a quarter of the poem. The words must be quoted in the context of 'criticism or review'.

Whilst this statement does not have the force of law, it carries considerable weight within the courts.

Poems, essays and other short works are treated as complete works, so permission is needed to copy these or any musical works.

Multiple copies of copyright material may not be made without prior permission, and payment may have to be made. If in doubt, you should ask the publisher of the work.

The law has become even tighter since a test case a few years ago was won by a music publisher against a local education authority who, it is alleged, photocopied large amounts of music and marked these as the education authority's property. If you find yourself photocopying scripts, be aware of copyright regulations. If in doubt, you can always request help from:

British Copyright Council
Copyright House
29–33 Berners Street
London W1P 4AA

When you intend to perform a play it is essential that permission is sought from the publisher and the writer's agent well in advance of any public announcements of the intended performance. The rights for a play can often be obtained from an accredited literary agent or through a society such as The Society of Authors or, in the case of a lot of amateur rights, Samuel French. For the professional rights of a play to be obtained a deal will have to be struck with the literary agent, which will depend on a number of factors, such as the length of run, the capacity of the theatre and the geographical position of the theatre. This fee may also be linked with a percentage of the box office takings.

For the reproduction of music there are a number of copyright agencies. The

Performing Rights Society Limited (PRS) is described as an association of composers, authors and publishers of music. This society guards the rights of its members' music. Most theatres will have a pre-negotiated fixed fee to cover the cost of reproducing music, payable at the beginning of each year to the PRS or PPL. The fee is fixed by a tariff kept by the Theatres National Committee and the Music Users Council, taking account of the location and the capacity of the venue. Phonographic Performance Limited governs the use of recorded music for things such as curtain up, interval and play out. A licence fee is payable in advance which is based on accurate returns made periodically which represent a list of all recorded material used. This method of return not only checks your fee but also looks after the interests of the musicians themselves.

It is to be remembered that the use of recorded music may be in question where:

- Musicians are regularly employed.
- An orchestra pit is part of the building and an orchestra could be used.
- A piece of music is not so much incidental but is more an integral part of the production.

Useful addresses

The Phonographic Performance Ltd
Ganton House
14–22 Ganton Street
London W1V 1LB

Performing Right Society Ltd
29–33 Berners Street
London W1P 4AA

Mechanical-Copyright Protection
Society
Elgar House
41 Streatham High Street
London SW16 1ER

Copyright Society of the USA
1133 Avenue of the Americas
New York
NY 10036

Appendix 3   Licences

Animals

Only the laws relating to the training and use of animals in performance are covered in this appendix.

The Performing Animals (Regulations) Act 1925 states that 'No person is to exhibit or train any performing animal unless registered under the Act.' By exhibit this means the use of any animal at an entertainment to which the public are admitted, whether paying or not. Local authorities keep registers and issue certificates as required, and local government officials and the police are notified so that they may inspect premises to ensure that conditions are being complied with. They will also ensure that the training or exhibition of performing animals is not being carried out cruelly.

The general law protecting animals, both wild and domestic, can be found in the Protection of Animals Act 1911, and later statutes dealing with particular animals and their use. It is under this Act that proceedings can be taken where the 1925 Act would be insufficient or inappropriate – for example, an entertainment where the public are not admitted, such as when an animal may appear in studios or on location for film productions.

As a test case when writing this book, I tried ringing the County Council in search of a certificate of performance. The gentleman I spoke to had never been asked to provide such a certificate before and requested time to read the legislation before he could decide whether a certificate would be required for the use of a domestic cat in Harold Pinter's *The Collection*. From his reply it appeared that the cat we intended to use was not 'a performing animal' and as such could only be regarded as a hand prop; a certificate was not regarded as necessary on this occasion!

Children

The use of children in performance is governed primarily by The Children (Performance) Regulations 1968, made under The Children and Young Persons Act 1963. These govern the appearance of children in entertainment and performances generally. Under Section 37 of the Act, every child must be licensed unless he performs four days or less in a six month period. There are still, however, regulations about unlicensed children.

Normally only children of 16 and under will be licensed. A child under 13 may be licensed if:

'The application is for acting and is accompanied by the employers' declaration that the part cannot be taken except by someone of the child's age.'

There are also clauses embracing the need for ballet dancing and musical skills in support of such an application. So in broad terms, a child will be granted a limit of not more than 6 days in performance or rehearsal and allowances must be made for education. For more information about this subject I would suggest you contact your local education authority.

WEAPONS

Firearms
As the violence in this world increases there is also growing aggravation attached to the sourcing and licensing of firearms for the theatre. It is, in short,

necessary to seek police clearance and a firearms certificate in order to have a theatrically effective weapon that goes bang. There are two main exceptions to this, purpose-built starting pistols and replicas. Legislation has for some time prohibited the possession of the following firearms in the UK:

Burst fire weapons
Self-loading rifles and carbines
Pump action rifles and carbines
Self-loading, smooth bore guns with barrels shorter than 24 inches
Pump action smooth bore guns with barrels shorter than 24 inches
Smooth bore revolver guns (except muzzle-loading guns and those chambered for 9 mm rim-fire cartridges)
Rocket launchers and mortars (except launchers for fireworks, signal flares and safety lines)
Any of the above weapons or any fully automatic gun which has been converted to a lower category

More recently there has been new legislation (February 1997) in the United Kingdom. An outline of the amendment to the Firearms Act was given by the Police Policy Directorate in the following way:

The Firearms (Amendment) Bill does not affect blank-firing pistols which are not readily convertible (i.e. those which do not require a Firearm Certificate). Among the reasons against imposing restrictions on such items in their use in theatres, cinema and television as a 'safe' alternative to real guns.

The general prohibition on the possession of real handguns will apply to those used for theatrical purposes. It would clearly be anomalous to prohibit the use of these items for target shooting, but permit their use for purposes where a fully-working gun is not needed. As handguns will become 'Section 5' prohibited weapons, they would fall under the same arrangements as apply at present to real machine guns. As you will know, there are companies which are authorised by the Secretary of State to supply such weapons for theatrical purposes.

The exemption under Section 12 of the Firearms Act 1968, whereby actors can use firearms without themselves having a Firearm Certificate, will remain in force.

If you have a specific need for a firearm in a theatrical situation I would suggest that you contact both the firearms department at New Scotland Yard and a professionally accredited supplier of weapons, such as Bapty.

Weapons that have been converted to a lower category of control will, to all intents and purposes, remain a prohibited weapon. Technically the conversion makes no difference to this. In other words, any converted weapons keeps its original prohibited status.

If a shot gun is to be used onstage, a shot gun licence will, without doubt, be required. If the weapon is to be fired then this adds another dimension to the problem. In practical terms, shot guns have very poor safety catches, for they are intended to be carried broken, that is, open without the cartridges in them. There are, however, two sorts of blank cartridges available for them. The first is a traditional twelve bore shot gun blank that is rather like a very short shot gun cartridge. The report from such a blank is extremely loud and better suited to the 1812 Overture. There are, however, shot gun blank adapters which fit into the breach of

a twelve bore shot gun but enable you to fire a .38 or .22 cartridge, which is not so loud and has less blast. When dealing with starting pistols, replicas and of course, real firearms, there are a number of precautions that must always be adhered to:

1 The gun must never be left unattended, loaded or unloaded on a prop table. It must be loaded just before it is to be used and handed to the actor as he goes on. It must then be taken from him immediately he comes offstage. The blanks must be counted in and counted out into a rack format cartridge box.

2 No gun should ever be pointed at anyone, even in jest, unless it has been blocked by the director and agreed if necessary by a specialist in that field.

3 Guns must be locked up after use and, where possible, taken apart. This allows the moving parts to be locked in one safe and the solid parts in another.

4 Ensure when using a starting pistol that the person handling it is absolutely clear as to the source and direction of the blast before it is fired. It is very common for the blast to come from the top of a starting pistol and the gun must therefore be held in the air to be certain that it is well away from the face of the operator and the faces of others.

Swords
Swords have not yet come under governmental licensing and they are an extremely effective theatrical device if used under professional supervision. A lot of drama schools now issue a certificate of proficiency to those who have participated in fencing classes. This does not make the holder of such a certificate a fight director, however.

There are three types of sword used in athletic fencing, the épée, the foil and the sabre. Most of the reconstructed period weapons available use an épée blade as the core of the weapon. For the purposes of setting a fight it may be possible to source épées that can be used in the rehearsal period from a school, college or local group. It may be necessary however, to improvise a frog and belt for these rehearsals.

In performance you must ensure that you have sufficient spare blades and have worked out a contingency plan for a sword breaking in performance. Before every performance there should be a fight call and a separate rehearsal conducted for the fight scenes. The swords themselves must be checked for wear and tear every night. An excellent book on this subject is *Fight Direction* by William Hobbs.

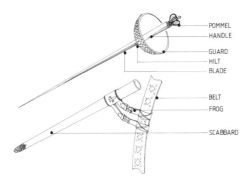

POMMEL
HANDLE
GUARD
HILT
BLADE
BELT
FROG
SCABBARD

Appendix 3 Sword and scabbard

Appendix 4   Paints and Glues

In stage management I found myself coming into contact with paints and glues of all kinds: painting props, touching up scenery, sticking prop dressing down or even sticking the sole back on to the leading lady's shoe. If you find yourself involved in the application of paints and glues it can also fall to the stage manage-ment to organize the removal of such things. In this instance a knowledge of solvents can be extremely useful.

All in all, a basic understanding of this area of work must be regarded as essential. Here, as originally conceived by David Lewis in his teaching days at London's Central School of Speech and Drama, is a resumé of paints and glues currently in use. Materials are expensive, so *do not waste them.* If you do mix up too much dye/paint etc. don't throw it away – label the jar, stating what it is, so that someone else can use it.

Paints

Water paints

The paints in the painting area of the stage workshop are pure pigment (colour). If they are mixed only with water they will flake off when dry. They must have a medium (binder) added to them. The two most common mediums are glue size and emulsion PVA (poly vinyl acetate). Glue size can be mixed with hot water.

Preparation of hot water glue size
Glue size comes in two forms, as small brown sugar-like granules, and as a stiff jelly (known as jelly glue size). To make hot water glue size both forms must be diluted with water and heated in a bucket, placed within an outer bucket which also has water in it. Never put the size bucket directly on the gas; the size will burn and form a useless foul-smelling black char-coal. The bucket will also be rendered use-less. For paint mixing the standard mix is approximately 1lb/.45 kg of size granules to a gallon/4.55 litres of water.

Preparation of paint, using glue size

Take a quantity of pigment (no more than you need for the specific job). Add water, mixing thoroughly until it is the consistency of double cream. Do not add pigment to water because you cannot judge the quantity accurately, and the pigment floats on the water and does not dissolve.

Some particular pigments dissolve poorly – Geranium Pink is a good example. Such pigments need a very small quantity of methylated spirits to dissolve them.

When the pigment is mixed, add the size from the size bucket. Dilute the whole mixture with hot water until it is just thinner than single cream consistency. This paint can only be used while it is hot or warm; when it cools down it jellifies. When painted on a surface it dries hard.

'Over-sized' paint glistens and cracks when dry. It will also warp the flats, and either tear or pull the canvas off them. 'Under-sized' paint will not hold onto the canvas, and will brush off, smudge and cause dust. Paint should be the right consistency so that it both covers well and is not too thin, flaking off when dry.

As with all painting, a better result is always achieved by painting more thin coats rather than less thick ones. Always allow the first coat to dry sufficiently before applying the next coat.

Scenic colours always dry lighter than when they are wet, so prepare your colours accordingly. Always test your colours on a small surface, and see the exact colour when dry.

Painting scenery with sized paint

All new flats should be 'primed'. This is the equivalent of an undercoat. The priming coat should correspond to the final colour, e.g. if your final colour is to be *black* either use a thin coat of plain size or black, do not use any white.

Depending on the effect required, there are a number of ways of painting scenery:

STIPPLING with a fairly dry brush, using the ends of the bristles and stippling, not stroking, on the paint.

SPLATTERING the canvas with paint, carefully flicking thin paint to achieve a speckled effect.

SPONGE WORK using a sponge, dabbing the paint onto the canvas.

DRY BRUSH WORK using an almost dry brush, dragging it across a dry canvas.

GLAZING, building up colour by a number of layers of thin paint which produces a translucent quality.

'Laying in' is a term used for blocking in areas of colour for a cloth or scenery, as you would with an undercoat. When painting a flat coat, the brush should go in all directions, to ensure that the paint fills all the pores of the canvas. Never scrub the paint onto the canvas: it ruins the brush and drags paint from underneath to the surface. This is very important when painting over previously painted flats.

Wash brushes out with hot but not boiling water. If left, the size in the paint will go 'off', producing a foul smell. Two or three teaspoonfuls of carbolic acid may be added to a bucket of paint, which will make it last longer.

Preparation of paint using PVA

Take a quantity of paint (no more than you need for the specific job) and add water, mixing thoroughly until it is the consistency of double cream. Then add PVA which has been diluted with water to the consistency of single cream. Dilute the whole mixture with water until it is just thinner than single cream consistency. It follows that the more pigment is used, the more PVA is required. Wash brushes out in warm, not hot water. If this mixture is to be kept for a length of time, it must be kept in a sealed airtight container, otherwise it will dry off and harden.

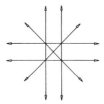

Appendix 4 Paint directions

Other forms of water bound paints

EMULSION PAINTS have trade names, and are sometimes called vinyl emulsion. Vinyl means that it contains a vinyl, usually poly vinyl acetate, normally known as PVA. These paints are virtually the same as pigment mixed with PVA but smoother as they are industrially blended and mixed. The smallest quantity you can buy is normally ½ litre. For your purposes, only buy cheap paint. Brushes should be washed in water.

POWDER PAINTS such as those made by Rowney or Reeves have already got a binder (medium) added. So all you need to do is add water.

POSTER PAINTS cover well on dark paper, card, etc. They are bought already mixed with water, and go hard if the lid is left off. Good for model making.

DESIGNERS' GOUACHE is a water based paint which is bought in tubes. Good colours, very expensive paints, and particularly useful when painting models and costume designs. As with all paints, some colours are more expensive than others, choose carefully. If carefully kept, these paints will last well.

POLYMER OR CRYLA PAINTS are waterproof plastic type paints, which are of very little use.

FLUORESCENT PAINT has a glow finish. It is good for signs.

Oil bound paints

There are many types of oil bound paint, but most common are the household gloss paints, including high gloss, and 'wet look' enamel paints. There is also eggshell, a semi-gloss paint with a finish rather like an eggshell. Undercoats for gloss paint and polyurethane may also be useful.

The advantages of these paints are that they are very durable and waterproof, and some good strong colours can be bought. They are expensive.

The solvent for these paints is turpentine or white spirit. Genuine turpentine is very expensive, and it is unnecessary to buy this. White spirit is most economically bought in large quantities. Brushes should be washed in turps substitute or white spirit until the paint has dissolved, then washed with warm soapy water and rinsed with clean warm water.

A large range of spray aerosol paints can now be bought, which are very useful for certain jobs. Read the instructions on the can carefully. A spray can should be held at least one foot away from the article being sprayed. Apply a thin coat, allow that to dry, then another until the surface is covered. Do not try to hurry this process. A common fault is to hold the spray too close to the article; the spray does not diffuse at so close a range, and a build-up of paint develops which runs and takes hours to dry.

When your job is finished, turn the aerosol can upside down. Depress the nozzle until all paint stops being sprayed, which will clear the nozzle. Then store.

PAINT STRIPPERS

There are two paint strippers widely available in the United Kingdom which will strip oil-bound paints, sold under the trade names of Polystripper and Nitromors. Nitromors is the stronger.

Both solvents contain nitric acid and burn if they come into contact with skin, especially broken skin. If they are accidentally splashed into the eyes, they should be washed out immediately with cold water, for a long time. If burning continues, see a doctor.

When using paint strippers, you should wear rubber gloves. If using a stiff brush, wear goggles. If the stripper gets splashed on clothes, wash it off immediately with cold water.

Dyes – water and spirit

Water dyes are used for fabrics. Spirit dyes are used for wood, metal, plastic, leather, enamel, etc.

Owing to the shellac varnish used in the spirit dye solution, spirit dyes are not in fact good for fabric, but it is still possible to paint onto fabric with spirit dye. Spirit dyes are very strong, and only a very small quantity is needed. Always test a small piece of material out first before using it on the actual thing.

Preparation of water dyes

Take a small quantity of dye (better to take a small quantity and keep adding than to take too much and try to dilute). Mix it in a jar with warm water until it has dissolved. Then pour slowly into hot water, and stir. Add glauber salts which are a fixative and come with the dye when it is purchased. (The dye will wash out if these salts are not used.) Common salt may be used if the article will not need to be washed. To test that you have the right colour, squeeze a small piece out thoroughly and dry. Now boil the dye up and having previously thoroughly soaked the material, immerse it into the boiling dye solution. Keep the material moving. When you have arrived at the right density of colour remove the articles from the dye solution and rinse in warm water.

Never mix more dye than is required for the job in hand.

A number of water dyes are widely available, and are listed here:

Dylon – a trade name, make a varied range of dyes, and you can check which dye is most appropriate for the material you are using. Read instructions on the tin, and follow them. A cold water Dylon is marketed too.

Dygon – (again a trade name) will bleach out colour to a certain extent, but usually not all the way. Bleach is better, but stronger, and will rot certain kinds of material.

Preparation of spirit dyes

Take a small quantity of spirit dye and dilute it with a small quantity of methylated spirit. When dissolved, add a small quantity of shellac varnish, and dilute to the required strength with methylated spirits. This substance is sometimes known as French enamel varnish or FEV and can be bought already made up in pint-sized bottles, at great expense.

After use, wash brushes with methylated spirits immediately, and then rinse them with water.

Wood dyes and stains

These can be bought in shops and are basically spirit dyes. They are expensive and unnecessary, as you can make them up yourself with spirit dye, shellac and methylated spirit, as described above.

Silver and gold powders

These are metallic powders and are very expensive. They should be mixed with shellac and methylated spirits and used sparingly.

Brushes

The first thing to remember about brushes is that they are very expensive, and if not treated carefully can become useless immediately. Always wash them out after use with the right solvent. Then rinse with warm (not hot) soapy water, and rinse again in water. If you use boiling water you will kill the bristle and the brush will go limp and useless.

Remember

Water paints emulsion size and pigment mixtures; wash with water.

Oil paints gloss, eggshell, undercoat, lacquer, polyurethane; wash with turps, then warm soapy water and rinse.

Spirit dyes first methylated spirit, then warm soapy water and rinse.

The following tips should be helpful:

1 Never use brushes with Copydex glue
2 Old brushes can *sometimes* be restored with 'Polyclens' (trade name)
3 Never put a brush in a bucket/tin which is on the gas
4 Always use the right size brush for the job.
5 Never stand a brush on its bristles, it bends them and renders them useless
6 Always think before you clean a brush, to make certain you are using the right solvent
7 Always clean your brushes immediately after use
8 Hang your brushes up after use

Glues or Adhesives

For good results, you must use the right adhesive. A variety of glues are described below; some are particularly appropriate for certain jobs, so find out as much as you can about them. A contact adhesive is one which needs to be applied to both surfaces of the material thinly, allowed to dry or become tacky, and then the two surfaces pressed together.

Emulsion glaze

Emulsion glaze is a thinned out form of poly vinyl acetate (PVA). Many PVA glues are sold under trade names: Marvin, Medium, Woodworkers, Resin W etc.

This is the most versatile glue, and can be used for anything from cement to tissue paper, depending on the strength. It can be diluted with water. When thick, it will stick wood, metal (up to a point), china, glass, cork, heavy card, etc. When thinned, it will stick paper, cloth and other light materials. When thinned more, it will act as a glaze and can be painted onto most surfaces to produce a shine or glaze.

Pearl glue or woodworkers' glue

This looks like brown pearl barley, and should be slightly diluted with water and heated in a bucket/tin placed within an outer bucket of water. Never put it directly onto gas. It is a very strong glue when dry, and will stick wood; it is also good for polystyrene, and for sticking rough cloth to wood (e.g. sacks, hessian to wood). A dirty glue to use.

Glue size

Glue size comes in two forms, either in small brown sugar-like granules, or a stiff jelly (jelly glue size); both forms should be diluted with water and heated in a bucket within another bucket of water. Never put it directly onto gas. If you do the size will burn and form a foul-smelling useless black treacle. It is good for sticking canvas to wood, wood to wood, and covering screws or nails with brown paper, hessian, etc.

Evostick (trade name)
A brown-rubbery glue (a contact adhesive which can be bought in tubes or tins. It is good for foam rubber, rubber, paper, cloth, and most light materials. Not a very clean glue to use.

Copydex (trade name)
A white latex rubber glue (a contact adhesive), which can be bought in tubes (too small) or tins from ½ litre to 2 gallons (better value). This is the best glue for fabric, but should be used very sparingly. It will stick all kinds of cloth, fabric, felt, underfelt, carpets, etc. It is, however, no good for smooth surfaces such as paper and wood.

Don't get it on your clothes as it won't come off. The manufacturers of Copydex make a solvent which can be obtained free by writing directly to them for a small bottle 'in case of accidental spillage'. By then it is too late. And that is the only solvent.

Never use a brush with Copydex. Use a wooden spatula, a palette knife, a piece of cardboard, rag, fingers – but never a brush.

Araldite (trade name)
An epoxy resin, which only glues when a chemical reaction takes place between the glue and the hardener. You mix the two tubes together in equal quantities. A very strong glue producing a rigid bond.

UHU (trade name)
A clear adhesive, good for model making and small jobs, with a slightly elastic quality. UHU also make a special balsa glue, which is excellent for model making.

Balsa cement
A clear adhesive, which dries brittle, for use only with balsa wood. It is good for model making.

Versifix (trade name)
A petroleum based glue, good for dry mounting pictures. As with Copydex, any excess can be rubbed off cleanly. It is expensive and not easily obtainable (made by Rexel products).

Gloy now make a similar petroleum based glue which is cheaper and can be bought in large quantities.

Prit (trade name)
A glue-stick, good for small paste-up jobs.

Spray mount (trade name)
A spray glue used for mounting paper onto board. As the glue doesn't dry immediately, the artwork or paper can be peeled off and repositioned if required.

Super Glue (trade name)
Just a little can produce a very strong rigid join. Not so good for flexible surfaces, but it will stick your fingers together if you are not careful.

Glossary

Act (a) To perform a role, as an actor. (b) Part of a play, ballet or opera.

Act drop The main or 'house' curtain which shuts off the stage from view.

Acting area The space on stage in which the action of the play occurs.

Acting edition Play text or script published after the original production which usually includes stage directions, lighting plot, property plot etc as in the first production.

Ad lib Freely invented dialogue spoken by an actor, often without approval.

Aisle Gangway between seat blocks in the auditorium.

Amp – abbreviation (a) Ampere – a unit of electrical current. (b) Amplifier – a piece of sound equipment.

Angel Colloquialism for a financial backer of a commercial presentation.

Apron See *Forestage*

Arbor (USA) American for counterweight cradle – see *Flying*

Asbestos (USA) See *Safety curtain*

Aside A line or speech spoken directly to audience and assumed by them to be unheard by the other characters in the play.

ASM Assistant Stage Manager.

Audition Trial hearing of an actor, singer etc seeking employment.

Backcloth (or Backdrop) Painted or plain cloth behind or upstage of setting.

Backer See *Angel*

Backflap A type of hinge frequently employed in scenery construction.

Backing Scenery which conceals backstage as viewed through a window, door etc.

Back lighting Lighting arranged to enhance modelling of actors from upstage or behind them.

Back projection See Projection

Back stage Area which is out of sight beyond the audience view of the scenery.

Back wall (a) The rear wall of the stage itself. (b) The rear wall of a box set.

Balcony See *Circle*

Band room Changing room and storage for musicians and their instruments.

Bar Usually a steel, iron or aluminium pipe suspended on ropes or wires to which may be fixed lighting equipment, scenery, etc.

Bar bells Bells in refreshment bars rung to signify the commencement of performance, usually operated by the stage manager.

Barndoors Removable shutters fitted to some types of lantern to limit or shape the beam of light.

Barrel (USA: Pipe) Steel, iron or aluminium tube attached to flying lines from which scenery etc may be suspended.

Batten (a) A length of timber used to join pieces of scenery or to which the top and bottom of a cloth is fixed. (b) A compartmented lighting unit of three or four circuits used to light large vertical areas such as backcloths etc.

Batten pocket Flat or tubular pocket sewn into the bottom of a cloth into which timber or metal may be fitted to give a straight edge to cloth.

Beginners See *Half*. Beginners are the first actors on stage in a scene.

Benefit A performance from which the proceeds may be given to an individual or a charity.

Billing material Contractually agreed size and position of names of performers.

authors, composers, directors, designers etc. Size is usually referred to or expressed as a percentage proportion of the size of the lettering of the title of the work being performed.

Billy block A pulley on a short length of rope used to divert the pull of a working rope, or to suspend a single item in storage.

Blackout (a) Complete absence of light on stage, for effect. (b) Black garments worn by stage staff to render them undetectable when working in little or no light.

Blinder Brilliant light or object used to temporarily 'blind' an audience and prevent their seeing something.

Block Frame in which one or more pulley wheels (or sheaves) are mounted – see *Flying*.

Blocking Initial organizing of actors' moves and positions in rehearsal – noted by the stage management in the prompt script.

Bomb tank See *Pyrotechnics*: usually a converted galvanized water tank.

Book ceiling Scenery ceiling folded for storage when flown.

Book flat Two-fold piece of scenery, to ease handling. Hence 'to book', fold.

Boom Steel, iron, or aluminium pipe mounted vertically to which lighting equipment etc. may be secured. Uusually with plate at foot and safety pick-up line suspension at top.

Border Soft or framed piece of material or scenery to conceal that which is above the set.

Boss plate Metal plate with threaded hole let into stage into which a machined screw locks as a means of locating and fixing a piece of scenery.

Box set Realistic scenery representing the interior of a room – a chamber set.

Brace (a) In the structure of a flat, an angled piece of timber. (b) Support for scenery on stage: (i) Extendable or telescopic (ii) French: built from timber.

Brace weight Cast iron weight placed on foot of extendable or French brace to prevent movement.

Brail Ropes so tied as to hold one or more pieces of scenery clear of others in the fly tower space over the stage.

Breakaway Prepared or specially made prop intended to be smashed or broken in the action of a play: capable of restoration for reuse. Some plastic and sugar-glass products are referred to as breakaways but are not capable of restoration.

Breast line A form of brail fixed at both sides of the stage or fly tower and running across the width of a flat so as to brail it.

Bridge Fixed or mobile, narrow walkway giving access to lighting and loudspeaker positions above the stage or the auditorium.

Bridge lift Rectangular lift in stage floor running SL to SR.

Bridle Short length of rope used to spread the loading on a flying line.

Business (a) Pantomimic action of the actor. (b) Financial state of success, or failure, relative to the show.

Cable Temporary, flexible electrical wiring used on stage to supply the lighting equipment. Also sound wiring.

Call a) Written or verbal instruction to actors and/or staff to standby or to attend for work, travel, costume fittings, etc. (b) The period of work etc to which the above call refers.

Call board Notice board on which calls are posted.

Call boy Largely obsolete term for person sent to 'call' actors for scenes – in most cases superseded by paging systems.

Cans Slang for intercoms.

Canvas Material used to cover scenery frames before painting.

Carpet cut A concealed slot into which the front edge of stage cloth or carpet was trapped to make a firm and neat fixing – growing obsolete.

Carpet hoist (USA) See *Flying*: Counterweight system.

Catwalk Narrow access to equipment, purpose built but not necessarily spanning an area like a bridge.

Ceiling piece Ceiling for whole or part of box set.

Centre line (a) A datum line which divides the stage from back wall to front. (b) The middle of a 3 or 5-line 'set' of lines in a flying system; see *Flying*.

Chamber set See *Box set*.

Channel A control circuit in lighting or sound equipment.

Character (a) Qualities represented by the actor and belonging to role played. (b) Aged or eccentric roles, as distinct from ingénue or juvenile.

Check Reduction of lighting or sound level, operated smoothly.

Chief electrician Usually, the senior member of the stage lighting team.

Choreographer Dance director

Choreography Pattern of the dance as directed by the choreographer.

Circle A tier of seats above and separate from the stalls. A balcony.

Clear stage (a) Instruction given to actors and/or staff to leave the stage. (b) State of stage when emptied of scenery and props.

Clearing stick Long pole or bamboo rod used to fend-off flying objects when dealing with or preventing a *foul* (q.v.).

Cleat Wooden or metal fixing shaped for tying-off lines in flying or, on stage, when joining flats together.

Clew Ring or triangular metal piece which is used to join several wires to a single pulling wire. Commonly found on manually winched lines to spot-bars.

Cloth Plain or decorated, painted or dyed. Large piece of material. Commonly representing sky, landscape, or left neutral.

Cloth rack Wall-mounted horizontal pegs of large size along and on top of which rolled cloths can be stored.

Cloth trap Hinged panel in wall or floor through which rolled cloths can be passed when getting in or out, or for access to storage. Also seen in the front wall of a removal van to accommodate rolled cloths of greater length than the van body.

Colour Piece of material used to filter from a light source *all* but the colour of the filter itself: usually plastic sheet; may be glass or gelatine, hence 'gels'.

Colour frame Card or metal frame to hold filter, placed in front of the light source and held in guides.

Colour wheel Electrically or manually operated disc fitted to the front of a lantern, with several apertures enclosed with coloured filters to facilitate rapid changes of coloured light.

Commedia dell'arte Italian improvised comedy which flourished from 16th to 18th century.

Commercial A show where risk capital is intended to be recovered, plus profit, as distinct from non-commercial which implies state, local or other subsidy or guarantee against loss.

Company manager The 'management' in the field, on tour etc, as in the West End. The backstage administrator in the subsidized/resident theatre. NOTE: Titles can be misleading and rarely mean the same in two different institutions. See also *Production Manager*.

Contour curtain Either a main or house curtain or other decorative curtain whose bottom-edge shape can be varied by remote control. Popular in the United States, rare in Britain.

Corpse Inadvertent laughter by an actor. Also called breaking-up: commonly caused by nervousness.

Costume parade See *Dress parade*

Counter weight See *Flying*

Cradle Part of counterweight – see *Flying*.

Cross fade Result of simultaneously increasing brightness of some lighting while reducing other.

Crossover A backstage or understage passage from side to side.

Cue (a) Word or action taken by one actor as signal to speak or move by another. (b) Signal given by stage management for action by actors or staff.

Cue board Panel of switches etc operated by stage management to 'give cues'.

Curtain (a) Drapery used to cut off view of stage or to decorate it. (b) Verbal cue to raise or lower the main or house curtain.

Curtain call Actors' acknowledgement of applause at end of play.

Curtain line Marked on ground plan to

show where curtain touched the stage.

Cut To delete from script. Also to bypass some text or action in rehearsal (deliberately, to save time: accidentally in performance).

Cut cloth (USA: Cut drop) Scenery cloth from which part has been removed according to the design, often to represent woodland.

Cut out Usually free-standing piece of scenery of plywood or other board, cut to shape of object depicted but flat, with no thickness.

Cut to cue Time-saving method of rehearsing technicalities by avoiding long passages of dialogue.

Cyclorama Usually a large cloth painted and set on curved mountings to simulate sky. In Europe it is common for the cyclorama to run on a track round the whole stage reaching from the proscenium on one side and meeting it on the other.

'D' lift Forestage area, often shaped like a 'D' that can be lowered to form an orchestra pit.

Dance captain Nominated senior or 'lead' member of dance team.

Dark Shut, closed-down: 'a dark theatre'.

Date A theatre or hall in which a show has been booked to perform. Used from the point of view of the show and its personnel.

Dayman Notwithstanding sex-discrimination legislation, a backstage person whose employment includes work done in daytime, i.e. additional to evening performance.

DBO Dead blackout. Totally dark: conventionally achieved by use of a master blackout switch.

Dead (a) Position agreed to which an object moves on cue. (b) Something which is no longer required, either temporarily or permanently.

Dead line A line fixed so as to arrest an object at the required point in its travel: usually added to suspended objects for safety.

Deading cleat An extra cleat on the fly rail for pre-setting a 'dead' position.

Designer One who designs scenery, costumes, lighting or sound in consultation with the director.

Dim To fade lighting to darkness or blackout, smoothly.

Dimmer Electrical or electronic equipment which varies the electricity supplied to a lamp so as to increase its brightness or dim it.

Diorama Infrequently used: a moving or rolling back cloth.

Dip Moment of relative or actual darkness in a Cross Fade: capable of avoidance when operating manually but increasingly avoidable by use of a Dipless cross fade feature in lighting control design.

Dip trap Metal or wooden plate in stage, usually hinged, beneath which are stage lighting socket outlets.

Director One who guides and advises actors so as to realize the whole presentation of a play. His artistic decision is usually final excepting cases where an overall director of productions or a commercial manager/producer has reserved the right to arbitrate the ultimate artistic decisions.

Distortion Unpleasant and inartistic result of bad recording, mishandled playback or faulty sound equipment.

Dock See *Scene dock*

Door slam Timber frame fitted with heavy door and bolts and locks used to simulate slamming door and other effects.

Double (a) 'Identical' performer e.g., acrobat 'doubling' for an actor in pantomime. (b) Playing two parts in the same play. (c) Historically Joe Grimaldi set a fashion for 'doing the double' by performing at Sadler's Wells then running to Covent Garden to give another performance. Later emulated (by car) by music hall artists.

Downstage Forward, towards the audience.

Drapes Stage curtains.

Drencher Sprinkler pipe fitted above the back of house curtain to soak it as a barrier in the event of fire outbreak backstage.

Dress parade Review by director, designer, costume/wardrobe staff, of all costumes worn by cast and paraded in (usually) stage lighting. Any defects, mis-fits etc are noted and rectified before the dress rehearsal.

Dress rehearsal See *Rehearsal*

Dressing (a) Decoration of a stage setting – any object which is not specifically a prop handled by the actor. (b) Assisting an actor in clothing himself. (c) Lighting on house curtain to enliven its appearance.

Drift Distance between flown object and flying bar to which it is attached by lines or wires – so calculated that the bar is unseen when the piece is *In* and the piece itself is out of sight when *Out*.

Drop (USA) See *Cloth*

Dry When an actor 'loses' or forgets his lines he is said to have *dried*.

Dry Ice Frozen CO_2 used for steam or 'smokey' effects, either on its own or in a machine.

Dry tech (USA) Cue-to-cue rehearsal without actors, for technical purposes only.

Dutchman (a) Wedge-shaped piece of wood to keep scenery upright when it is standing upon a raked stage; see *Rake*. (b) Strip of canvas or muslin stuck over a scenery joint and painted in to conceal it.

Effects Often abbreviated in notes, prompt scripts, etc as 'FX': describes sounds and visual detail, whether created 'live' or by recorded means.

Electrics Usually abbreviated to 'Elecs' or 'LX': a loose term which refers to almost anything electrical, including the staff.

Elevation A term in draughtsmanship: Plan: a vertical 'bird's eye' view. Elevation (front, end or rear): object viewed at eye level. Section: a view taken upon a hypothetical cutaway.

Elevator See *Lift*.

End stage See *Stage*.

Entr'acte Interval music, live or recorded.

Entrance The act of entering to play a scene.

Epilogue Speech or short poem addressed by actor to audience at the end of a play: common in the classics.

Equity Abbreviation of British Actors' Equity: the trade union which organises and negotiates on behalf of actors, directors, designers and stage managers.

Exit (a) the act of leaving a scene, (b) the way out for the audience.

Extras Additional performers without lines to speak – more usually in films or television. Used to be called *Supers* (Supernumaries): employed for crowd scenes.

Fade In theatrical usage refers to smooth increase or decrease of light or sound. Hence *Fader*: that part of the equipment which performs the function.

False Proscenium Inner proscenium, often decorated to match actual proscenium.

False stage Additional stage thickness for a show, frequently used in musicals etc to accommodate drives and wires for moving effects.

Felt Used to soften the tread of feet on rostrum or stair tread – ordinary carpet underfelt applied before canvassing.

Festoon (a) Another word for *Swag*, (q.v.). (b) Refers to Festoon Curtain or Tabs which adopt a sculpted shape.

Finale Conclusion of a play or, more commonly a musical or pantomime, when all the cast take part. Often leads directly to the curtain calls.

Fire proofing Treatment to retard inflammability.

First night Traditionally the first performance, at which critics are present. Also see *Preview*.

Fish plate Sometimes used to mean a plywood piece glued and nailed across the joint of a flat. May be employed instead of cut joint.

Fitting A 'call' for an actor to attend for the purpose of trying on costumes or wigs, etc.

Fit-up (a) First time of setting up scenery. (b) Traditionally a branch of touring theatre in which brief visits and one-night stands were played. (c) A temporary stage structure complete with suspension gear.

Five See *Half*.

Flame effect Flame on stage created by means of a variety of tricks or illusions.

Flash An effect produced by (a) Electric light

switched briefly, (b) *Pyrotechnics*, (q.v.). Also verbal instruction when lighting designer wishes to identify a particular lantern's contribution in cue.

Flat Conventional flat piece of scenery made of timber framing, canvas covered, primed and painted. In some companies and drama schools flats are reused by washing down and repainting.

Flicker wheel Electrically or manually operated disc fitted at the front of a lantern in which are holes. The disc being rotated thereby causes the beam of light to flicker.

Flipper A narrow hinged piece of scenery. When positioned it usually completes a setting by, for example, linking a set on a revolve with the permanent part of the set on the main stage.

Float Let a flat fall to the stage from the vertical so that air cushions its fall.

Floats Early form of *Footlights*, q.v. Burning wicks in oil. Many people still use the term *Float* when referring to Footlights.

Flog To remove charcoal or chalk sketch-lines from a piece of painted scenery, with a flogger made from a stick to which are attached several strips of clean fabric, e.g., strips of canvas.

Flood Type of lantern used to flood light on to a cloth or backing. It has a reflector and no lens.

Floor cloth See *Stage cloth*.

Flower path Loosely translated from the Japanese *Hanamichi* – a narrow platform extending from the stage into the auditorium, used for entrances and exits in the Kabuki theatre.

Fluff An actor's mistake on text, not a dry, but a muddle.

Fly floor Gallery at the side of the stage from which the flying system is operated.

Flying Causing objects or people to move through the air vertically or horizontally, under controlled conditions.

The original system for flying scenery comprised ropes which led from the fly floor upward and over a head block (multiple pulley diverter) and thence to single sheaves below which the ropes were attached to the flown object. The latter pulleys are the short – nearest the fly floor, centre – centre stage, and long – furthest. The ratio of effort required to operate by the *Flymen* (operators) is 1:1.

Separate sets of flying *Lines*, or single lines, additional to the basic system installed are called Spot lines and are placed where needed.

Many theatres are equipped with *Counterweight flying systems*. The flown object is usually attached to a bar which itself is suspended on steel wires. The wires pass over sheaves back to the side wall. There the wires are attached to a cradle which slides up and down the wall in guides or tracks. The cradle is loaded with iron or lead counterweights to balance the load. Normally one flyman can operate a well-balanced set by hauling up and down on an endless line.

Counterweight systems are either single purchase (ratio 1:1) or double purchase (ratio 1:2).

'Assistance' may be added to any flying system by rigging additional lines, pulleys and sandbags. One particularly useful additional rig is known as a carpet hoist (USA) which permits the flown object to be removed from the system temporarily – e.g., for a scene – while the principal counterweight cradle is supported by means of an overhaul.

The flying of people as in *Peter Pan*, or on cloud machines as in the classical *Deus ex Machina* can be performed using regular counterweight sets or modified versions but is not altogether recommended. Special rigs are commonly used and there are specialist suppliers.

Fly plug Stage lighting socket outlet located on or near the fly floor.

Fly rail One side of the fly floor is usually fitted with a heavy steel or timber rail to which cleats are fitted, on which flying lines are tied-off.

Fly tower Upper part of the space above the stage (stage house – USA). Preferably not less than 2⅔ times the height of the maximum opening of the *Proscenium* (q.v.) in order to allow flown items to pass out of sight of the audience.

Focus In stage lighting the term is used to refer to aiming, setting beam size and shape of lanterns.

Follow spot A powerful spotlight usually fitted with its own dimmer, iris and shutters which is mounted in a convenient position in or above the auditorium. Operated by a member of staff it is used to light individual performers wherever they move on stage. Common in musical comedies, ballet, ice shows, tattoos, etc.

Footlights A compartmented batten recessed into the front edge of the stage, used to illuminate the actors' faces. Modern techniques in lighting and make-up render footlights virtually obsolete.

Forestage That part of the stage which projects from the proscenium into the auditorium.

Forward Downstage, toward the auditorium.

Foul An entanglement of lines, scenery and/or lighting equipment in the flies.

Framed cloth A cloth to which vertical side and centre timers have been added to make it rigid.

French brace See brace.

French flat or Frenchman Several flats battened together to fly as a complete wall.

Fresnel A 'stepped' lens which produces a soft-edged beam, after the inventor.

Fresnelite (USA) Spotlight fitted with a fresnel lens.

Front Colloquialism for auditorium. 'Playing front' means direct to audience.

Front cloth Commonly in musicals and revues, a cloth flown closely behind the proscenium in front of which short scenes are played while big changes of scenes are carried out behind, or upstage.

Front of house Abbreviated to 'FOH': anywhere but backstage, such as foyers, bars, box office, auditorium, etc.

Frost Opalescent or translucent filter medium used in lighting to diffuse a beam of light.

Full house Sold out.

Fullness Draperies made up with deep 'gatherings' have fullness – usually requiring not less than 50% additional fabric, measured at head and foot.

Fusible link Usually a solder link in a chain or wire that melts and fails in the event of fire so as to release automatically a *Lantern* (Haystack) Smoke Flap or Safety Curtain.

Gantry A gallery or catwalk giving access to equipment, usually high level.

Gauze Material used in costume, props and scenery making. Often used for visual effect called *Bleed through* (slow) or *Transformation* (fast) when a picture painted on the downstage side is lit it is seen, but when light is introduced upstage the picture disappears.

G-clamp Ironmongery fitting for attaching a lantern to a bar.

Gel Abbreviation for *Gelatine*. See *Colour*.

Get-in The act of, or the location of the door for taking scenery etc into a theatre.

Get-out Removal of scenery, etc, from a theatre.

Ghost (a) Extraneous light hitting an object: often result of poor focusing. (b) Traditionally the 'ghost walked' on Friday when the company was paid.

Ghoster Slang for working an 'all-nighter'.

Glass crash (a) Sound of breaking glass. (b) Effects box made up specially to contain broken glass used for the effect.

Go (a) Verbal instruction to perform an action or a cue. (b) Word written in prompt script indicating where cue is given.

Gobo Metal plate cut or etched to produce a design which is then projected by a spotlight – most commonly a foliage pattern.

Gods Traditionally, the gallery or highest level of seating.

Grave trap See *Traps*.

Green Colloquialism for the stage.

Green room A space with or without refreshment facilities set aside for actors to use when awaiting rehearsal or performance calls.

Grid (USA – Gridiron) Timber or metal 'floor' of beams or perforated sheet, close to the top of the fly tower to which, or above which, the pulleys of the flying system are attached. Also the point from which dead lines are set up.

Grommet (a) A rubber or brass 'bush' lining a cable entry to a box to prevent cable chafe. (b) Ironmongery fitting to hold a line tight to the back of a piece of scenery, especially when flying.

Ground cloth (USA) See *Stage cloth*.

Ground plan A scale drawing in map form of a stage and/or scenery and furniture.

Ground row (a) A piece of scenery (a 'cut out') which usually represents the horizon, set at the foot of a cloth or sky, and often conceals the following: (b) compartmented lighting batten used to illuminate the bottom of a sky or designed cloth.

Group A selection of lighting or sound channels brought under one control.

Half The 35 minutes before the advertised beginning of a performance. *Half an hour* is called 35 minutes beforehand, *Quarter* is called 20 minutes beforehand, *Five* is called 10 minutes beforehand, *Beginners* is called 5 minutes beforehand.

Ham Ineffective, or over-acting.

Hand props See Properties.

Hanging iron Ironmongery fitting fixed at bottom of flown flat to which is tied the suspension line.

Head block Multiple block of sheaves over which the flying system lines first pass to divert them to their own individual short, centre and long sheaves or *Loft blocks*. *Head block* – sheaves are fitted one above another. *Lead block* – sheaves are side by side. Either may be found in manual flying systems. In a counterweight system a multiple grooved sheave *Lead block* is normal.

Heads below Shouted warning from staff working overhead to indicate that some object such as a spanner has been dropped.

Heads up Shouted warning at stage level to look up, when scenery, etc, is being lowered.

Heel Rear bottom corner of a flat that is being *Run*, (q.v.).

Hemp set Colloquially a set of rope lines; hence a theatre may be known as a 'hemp house' as distinct from a 'counterweight house'. See *Flying*.

HOD Head of Department; e.g., Chief Electrician.

Hot spot Over-concentrated light creating a bright patch – needs refocusing or diffusing.

House (a) Colloquially, the audience at a particular performance. (b) Colloquially, the whole theatre building.

Housekeeper Person in charge of the cleaning and other 'domestic' arrangements in a theatre.

House lights (a) The auditorium lighting which is commonly faded out while the play performs. (b) Verbal instruction to fade the house lights up or down.

House lights out Verbal instruction to fade the house lights to blackout.

Image The 'picture' produced by use of a projector or gobo.

Improvisation Invented speech and/or action during an actor's training, during rehearsals or, in some cases, within a performance when required by the director.

In Colloquialism for down, see *Flying*.

Incidental music Music within the performance of a play used for dramatic or atmospheric effect, not as a sound effect.

Independent (a) An electrical power or lighting circuit which is totally separate from the stage lighting control. (b) A channel within the stage lighting control which has been temporarily switched to become independent of the rest of the channels which remain under control of the operator. *NOTE:* In both cases the purpose is to drive equipment without risk of loss of power.

Inner proscenium A specially built secondary proscenium positioned upstage of the architectural proscenium (false prosc.).

Inset Small stage setting – often an interior – set within a larger setting which is not removed.

Intake Incoming electricity supply to a building.

Intercom (Abbreviation) Commonly referring to microphone/headset receiver communications equipment.

Interior Chamber set.

In the round See *Stage*.

Iris diaphragm Adjustable aperture which varies the size of the beam of light.

Iron See *Safety curtain*.

Island set Stage setting isolated by unoccupied space around it.

Jack knife See *Stage*.

Jog Narrow piece of scenery usually set at right angles to those which are adjacent to it which brings the side walls of a box set closer together upstage to improve the Sightlines, (q.v.).

Keep alive Instruction to avoid 'burying' or 'losing' a piece of scenery etc because it will be needed again soon.

Kill To switch off (a light, etc): to strike (scenery, props etc).

Knuckle A fold as in a book flat.

Lantern (a) Sometimes known as 'haystack' because of its shape, a glazed section of roof over the fly tower which opens in case of fire. An up-draught is created which inhibits fire from spreading quickly towards the auditorium. Release is automatic by fusible link or deliberately by using an axe or knife on a *Cut-line*. (b) General term for unit of lighting equipment including spotlight, flood, etc. *NOTE:* Currently the trend is to employ the word *Luminaire* instead of lantern because of its international understanding.

Lash line (USA) See *Cleat*.

Lead block See *Head block*.

Left Stage direction: actor's or stage left: prompt side.

Leg A drapery or flat, either suspended or standing, set as masking piece at the side of the acting area. Usually set up in pairs across the stage.

Leg drop (USA) See *Cut cloth*.

Lekolite (USA) A profile spotlight – derived from the manufacturer's name. See *Spotlight*.

Length Colloquialism for a row of ordinary general service lighting 'bulbs' in batten holders mounted on a length of timber, and used to illuminate a backing.

Lens Optical glass, ground to fine limits, the purpose of which is to direct light.

Let in To lower.

Librarian Often a non-playing member of an orchestra or band whose responsibility is to store, issue and retrieve musical 'parts'.

Libraries Jargon term sometimes used to refer to ticket agencies.

Libretto Text of opera, or other long vocal composition.

Lift (a) Stage machinery: an *Elevator* or section of a stage which can be set to different positions above and below the stage level. May be hand-wound, commonly electrically driven, less usually (in Britain) hydraulic. (b) a dance movement usually carried out by the male dancer, lifting his partner.

Lifting jack Castored lever hinged to offstage side of a piece of scenery – when lever depressed, the castor operates to assist in moving the piece.

Lighting The process of illuminating the play, moment by moment according to mood, time of day, location, etc. Nowadays it is common to employ specialist lighting designers but most 'resident' companies depend upon a member of the staff combining lighting design with other duties. On tour the company or stage manager usually lights the play.

Lighting layout Drawing and supporting data which graphically describes the use of equipment.

Limber Warming-up exercises executed by actors and dancers prior to rehearsal or performance to prepare the voice and muscles.

Limelight An obsolete source of intensely bright light. The abbreviation *Limes* is often used to refer to *Follow spots*, (q.v.).

Line (a) A line of dialogue spoken by an

actor. (b) Verbal request by an actor needing a prompt. Generally considered to be bad practice, and discourteous. (c) Verbal instruction by director to stage manager to announce the appropriate dialogue for resumption of rehearsal after a stop. (d) Rope or cord. (e) In electrics: the live wire or supply.

Live (a) In electrics: the supply wire when connected to a supply which is 'on' (and dangerous). (b) In electrics: any piece of equipment that has a fault which causes it to be in a dangerous condition is called 'live'. (c) Any item of scenery etc which is required for use.

Load (a) The contents of a lorry or van having been packed with scenery, costumes, props, etc. (b) Electrically, the rating in watts of the equipment connected to a channel.

Loading gallery In a theatre equipped with counterweight flying it is customary to have at high level a gallery from which loading and unloading of the cradles is possible while the staff hold the bar at stage level.

Lock rail (USA) Rail at stage level on which are mounted rope locks which are designed to prevent a balanced counterweight set from moving.

Long line The line of a flying set which is furthest from the fly floor.

Luminaire Any unit of lighting equipment: the international term which is intended to replace *lantern*, (q.v.).

Lx See *Electrics*.

Make-off (USA & Nautical) See *Tie off*.

Make-up The variety of traditional *Greasepaints*, modern cosmetics and auxiliary materials used by actors to enhance or to alter their appearance under stage lighting.

A base or foundation is first applied to the skin over which colour, highlights, age-lines etc are added. Body make-up is required for some roles: traditionally wet white or modern liquid or pancake colour is used. Structural changes to the face may be made by using nose putty and the torso and legs may be changed by wearing forms of padding. In Britain actors do their own make-up under most circumstances in the theatre; in TV and film it is customary for make-up (and the expert staff to apply it) to be provided by the employer. The costume or wardrobe departments of theatres usually undertake any special requirements including body make-up.

Marie Tempest The name of a famous actress with whom a device was associated – a lockable adjustable door-stay.

Mark-out Position, full size, of scenery indicated on rehearsal room or stage floor for use in rehearsal.

Maroon Electrically-fired explosive device: see *Pyrotechnics*.

Mask (a) Worn or carried by actors for specialized effect. (b) Metal plate with a cut out shape to insert into a spotlight to alter the size of the beam of light which is emitted. (c) To conceal something from view: hence masking.

Master A principal control in lighting or sound which may be a switch, or a fader. Channels may be controlled individually, by a sub-master which takes a group, or by the master which controls all.

Master carpenter Traditional title of the person who is in charge of the technical running of the stage, and/or workshop.

Medium Sometimes used as an alternative when referring to colour filters.

Memory A function built in to some modern lighting controls which permits both storage and retrieval of information.

Mic Abbreviation for *Microphone*.

Milk Squeeze more curtain-calls than the reception warrants.

Mis-cue An accidental, wrongly-timed cue, or one in which the dialogue spoken is incorrect or incomplete.

Mixer A piece of sound equipment which facilitates the mixing of several sources of sound either for recording or during playback.

Model Scale representation of scenery as designed which is usually shown to the cast of a play at the first reading and is then handed over to the manufacturers and painters for their guidance.

Monkey-stick Piece of strip wood or cane taped to the cleat line to assist positive and rapid tying-off, particularly in an awkward corner.

Multiple set A style of stage setting in which the scenery incorporates panels and hinged pieces which move to a variety of positions to suggest differing locations. An alternative to using different sets.

Musical director In musicals and revues the conductor is usually given this title: abbreviated to 'MD'. During rehearsals he is responsible for co-ordination of all the musical content.

Notice (a) Criticisms published by the press are known as notices. (b) The notice is the management's advice to the cast of a play or to a resident company, that their contracts will 'cease and determine' after the performance at a particular date.

OP Abbreviation for *Opposite Prompt* – stage or actor's right.

Off (a) An actor is 'Off' when he is late for an entrance. (b) To 'Go Off' is to leave the stage. (c) *Offstage* is the opposite of being on.

On To 'Go on' is to make an entrance to the stage.

Open stage See *Stage.*

Open white Lighting in which no colour filters are used: very common nowadays owing to improved equipment, techniques, and can obviate the need of some actors wearing make-up.

Orchestra (a) Term usually used for any size or combination of musicians playing in an orchestra pit. (b) Orchestra pit is located between the front of the stage and the auditorium. (c) Orchestra stalls: an obsolescent term for the stalls nearest to the stage and not overlapped by a circle.

Out In flying, means up.

Out front In the FOH, or in the auditorium.

Outrigger waggon A wheeled structure fitted to the offstage size of scenery to facilitate easy movement, when viewed by the audience is unseen.

Overhaul A line rigged so as to remove the effect of a counterweight.

Override Facility for the operator to take over manually from an automatic function on lighting control.

Pack To place flats together against a wall or in any suitable place is to make a pack. Hence: live pack – wanted: dead pack – used.

Pageant Though obsolete many pageants are still used enthusiastically: a lantern without lens, fitted with spill rings, which preceded the modern beam light which has a parallel beam.

Paging Calling by means of microphone and loudspeakers. Hence, 'paging amp': the amplifier in the system.

Paint frame A structure to which flats are fixed and which enables the scenic artist to paint in the vertical plane. Some frames are fixed and the painters travel up and down with their palette on a mobile platform; some are rigged to travel electrically past the painters.

Panic bolt Quick release lock fitted to exit doors operated by pushing horizontal bar.

Papier mâché Traditionally used in prop and mask making, a material made from absorbent paper and paste. Laid in layers over a former; once dried the papier mâché is rigid and durable.

Part The actor's role. Hence the obsolescent term *Part-script* in which only the word cue was given for the actor's own dialogue. Today it is customary for each actor to have a full script.

Pass door Door separating FOH from backstage – used principally by management in performance.

Patch Some stage lighting and sound systems have a patch system, similar to a telephone exchange 'cord' instrument, which facilitates linking selected dimmers to channels where flexibility is necessary to overcome a deficiency of controls.

Pause The appropriate symbol is noted in the prompt script by the stage management when a pause is agreed so as to avoid an unnecessary prompt.

Pelmet Particularly, a flat or decorated fabric piece hung to conceal the safety curtain in its raised position.

Pepper's ghost A famous illusion, still used in some magician shows in which an actor is seen by the audience via an arrangement of mirrors.

Perch A platform located behind or within the proscenium from which lighting and/or sound effects may be directed.

Periaktoi Greek system of three-faceted scenery units, triangular in section, which turned to show decorated scenes, as required.

Period Any time in history which is not the present. A 'sense' of period is invaluable to actors and stage manager alike.

Permanent setting For a particular play, or a season of plays, a method of design which requires little or no alteration or addition.

Photo call A call made specifically for the purposes of taking photographs of a production, whether posed or taken while scenes are 'run'.

Picture stage See *Proscenium*.

Piece (a) A piece of scenery. (b) Colloquialism for a play.

Pin hinge A hinge from which the pivot pin has been removed and replaced by a loose pin, thus enabling two pieces of scenery to be joined or separated easily.

Pin rail (USA) Fly rail fitted with cleats – see *Flying*.

Pit (a) Obsolete term for rear stalls seats beneath a circle. (b) Abbreviated orchestra pit.

Plano-convex A type of lens.

Plant Heating, ventilation, air-conditioning equipment etc – hence plant-room.

Plate Abbreviation for *fish plate* (q.v.).

Platform (USA) See *Rostrum*.

Play 'til ready Descriptive of the orchestra playing repeats to cope with a hiatus caused by delay: e.g., if a scene change goes wrong.

Plot (a) The thematic structure of a play which may have subsidiary or sub-plots. (b) Lists of actions or objects: for example, fly-plot (cue by cue requirements), hanging-plot (what hangs on each flying set), prop plot (all the props in the play listing their settings), prop running plot (what happens to props, where they should be moved in changes etc.).

Point hoist Electrically driven single-line flying hoist which can be positioned where required by use of diverters.

Police light Some licensing authorities permit the installation of a switch which enables an almost perfect blackout to be achieved. But only on the understanding that the switch must be adequately supervised by management or staff. Hence: it is 'policed'. Another term in the past was Lord Chamberlain's switch.

Portal An archway made by combining wings and border.

Pounce Sheet of waxed or varnished card on which a design is drawn. The scenic artist pricks the line of design and can use the pounce as a stencil. The resulting pin marks are joined to reproduce the original. Usually adopted when repeating designs are needed.

Powered flying Not yet common in Britain. Examples: *Point hoists*, a counterweight systems with *Electrical power assistance*, and straightforward *Hydraulic* drive (most commonly found in Europe).

Practical (a) That which is usable by the actor: e.g., a window in scenery, a revolver which fires. Opposite of non-practical: e.g., a dummy revolver which does not have to fire. (b) Electrically, a usable, switchable lamp standard etc.

Practice skirt Long skirt worn by actresses during rehearsals to help familiarity with period movement etc.

Premiere Another term for *First night*.

Preset Facility in some lighting controls for preparing one or more cues in advance. Also refers to anything in position before the beginning of a scene or act.

Press Colloquialism for published reviews or criticisms.

Preview Performance played before the official first night. Reduced priced tickets may be sold. In the case of charity previews it is usual for tickets to be sold at enhanced prices in aid of the charity.

Primer A base coat of paint applied to new

scenery on which the final decoration is done.

Producer The manager who presents a show: he organises the financial backing, employs the director and cast, etc. There is sometimes confusion because at one time the producer (in Britain) was what we now call director.

Production The whole show is a production.

Production desk Ordinary or purpose-built table which may be fitted with its own lighting and telephone etc, at which the director and his production team sit during rehearsals.

Production manager Responsible for causing all the physical aspects of a show to be made and to work. In some companies he may also perform the duties of company manager.

Profile (a) Shaped edge of scenery, ground row etc. (b) In electrics a *Profile spotlight* is a lantern which throws a beam which is adjustable in shape and focus.

Projection Whether movie or still, projected images are most frequently from the front of the object or screen. When back projection is done special screen material is essential.

Prologue Preliminary discourse or introduction to a play spoken to the audience.

Prompt Word or line spoken loudly enough for the actor to hear and to help him resume his dialogue after a dry.

Prompt box Found in continental opera houses, down stage centre, enclosed by a hood or cowl: in which sat the 'Siffleur' (literally 'whistler').

Prompt corner The space from which control of the performance is exercised, fitted with cue-lights, desk for the prompt script, telephone, etc.

Prompt script 'The book' in which is the full text of the play and into which during rehearsals the stage management enter moves and stage business. During technical and dress rehearsals all the cues are added for the control of the show. Also prompt copy.

Property master Person in charge of props.

Property table Set in wings and used for no other purpose. Often marked by drawing silhouettes of objects to make checking easier.

Props Abbreviation for properties: the objects used and handled by the cast. Difficulty sometimes arises as to what is a prop but in general the rule is that furniture and small battery driven objects are props, together with crockery, books, etc whereas scenery, trees etc are not. *NOTE*: Rocks are props – usually!

Props otherwise are described by these terms: Set: pre-positioned such as furniture and furnishings. Hand: portable whether pre-set or ready on tables in the wings. Personal: issued to the actor in the dressing room and his more direct responsibility, such as watches, spectacles etc.

Proscenium 'The fourth wall': a picture frame through which the audience sees the play. A false proscenium is a secondary framing usually black but sometimes decorated to match scenery or architectural proscenium.

Proscenium doors 18th century access to forestage, often in line with boxes above – used by actors for scenes.

Pusher See *Run*.

Pyrotechnics Explosive or flammable effects. *NOTE:* All pyrotechnics are dangerous unless rules for safety are observed. Examples: *Maroon* – electrically fired explosion, used in 'bomb tank'. *Smoke* – generated by slowly burning powder on special effect plate with electrical heater, or vapourised 'oil' heated by electrical element and driven by CO_2 pressure. *Flash* and *Coloured fire* – electrically fired by special equipment and using powders or papers.

Q Sometimes used as an abbreviation for *Cue*.

Quarter See *Half*.

Quick change Speedy change of scenery, etc, or costume between two scenes.

Quick change room Permanent or temporary space in which actors make fast changes of costume and wigs when there is insufficient time for them to get to and from their dressing room.

Quick study Said of actor who can learn lines fast.

Rag Crude colloquialism for tabs or curtain.

Rail See *Flying*.

Rain box Contains dried peas or the like – when tipped sounds like rain.

Rake Permanent or temporary slope on a stage. Stages used to be built with a rake, nowadays they tend to be flat and the auditorium is raked to facilitate the audience's view. Stage machinery can be installed to provide variable raking positions.

Ramp Sloping scenery platform.

Reading (a) Process of examining scripts to decide whether they are worth producing, carried out by readers on behalf of managements. (b) Prior to rehearsals most directors have the cast read the play seated in a circle, so as to get the 'feel' of the piece.

Rear fold Type of curtain track which gathers the fabric from offstage instead of bunching at the leading edges when opening.

Reflector Glass, or more usually metal, which is optically correct to reflect light. In the case of spotlights and projectors the accuracy of the reflector is vital so that maximum light is directed through the lens.

Rehearsal Preparation of a play by practising the scenes. Often done in a room until the production period when the show comes to the stage. Then, after the fit-up and lighting will follow technical, stopping dress and full dress rehearsals.

Remote control Dimmers and amplifiers are usually placed at some distance from the operators who therefore use remote control.

Repertory Originally: a store house. Repertory: short straight runs of plays presented by a theatre. The connotation is if adopting repertoire (the French word for the same thing): a stock of dramatic or musical pieces which the company or performer is accustomed to perform.

Repetiteur Rehearsal pianist – term used mostly in opera and ballet.

Report Stage managers and heads of departments make reports giving the detail of times, absences, faults etc after each performance.

Resin box Tray of crushed or powdered resin used by dancers to reduce the risk of slipping on the floor.

Return (a) A *Thickness piece* in scenery which suggests the thickness of a wall at a doorway, chimney breasts, etc. (b) Financial statement made by the box office manager nightly and weekly, which is sent to the manager, director etc.

Reveal See *Return* – the built part which is often independent of the flat where the thickness of a door, window and arch are revealed.

Reverb. Abbreviation for reverberation. Echo effect which may be added to sound during recording or may be applied by an equipment facility within the control.

Revolve Permanent or portable stage machinery – a turntable on which scenery can be driven to different positions. Different designs include: plane disc, concentric rings, drum, two-tiered etc.

Rig Colloquialism for arrangement of wires, lines and equipment for flying scenery or the layout of stage lighting. Also the process of installing lighting, sound and general stage equipment.

Right Stage direction.

Ring down-up Colloquialism for cueing the main or house curtain.

Riser microphone Microphone on a stalk which is raised and lowered electrically or mechanically – stored beneath the stage.

Roller Bottom fitting with lines fitted to a cloth which has to be rolled up because of inadequate height in a fly tower.

Rolling Cyclorama A German invention where the cyclorama is fitted to a conical drum from which it is unrolled laterally and runs round the stage on a track.

Rope lock Device which prevents the counterweight/flying hauling line from moving in either direction.

Rostrum A rigid or collapsible scenery platform.

Royalty Percentage of gross income being the contractual entitlement in payment to a playwright, director, and sometimes actor.

Run (a) Period between first night and closure. (b) Move a flat in the vertical plane. The leading edge is lifted slightly (*Toe* up) by one stagehand who guides its direction. A second stagehand (*Pusher*) keeps the rear bottom corner (*Heel*) on the stage and applies the force for movement.

Running plot Detail of progressive movements required through a show in each department's work, props, lighting, sound etc. For operation, as distinct from a state plot.

Run out Planking or built platform set up for rehearsal in the theatre to enable people to cross back and forth over orchestra pit.

Run through A rehearsal of a complete show at the 'normal' performance speed.

Safety chain Licensing Authority requirement: chain fixed round saddle of lantern and suspension bar to prevent lighting equipment falling on audience in the event of failure of locking device.

Safety curtain Separates auditorium from stage in event of fire. Released manually or automatically the commonest form is 'guillotine' which slides at the back of the proscenium. Made of steel or asbestos sheet.

Safety lighting Battery/mains lighting sufficient to enable an audience to leave premises in the event of failure of normal lighting – as agreed by licensing authority.

Sand bag Weight attached to unused flying line to prevent its running back through pulleys. If filled with lead shot – known as shot bag.

Sandwich batten Two thicknesses of timber trapping the top or bottom edge of a cloth, with rounded corners to avoid damage when rolling the cloth.

Scenario Skeleton libretto of play or opera.

Scene Part of an act of a play.

Scene change Minor adjustment to denote passage of time, etc, or complete change of scenery to change location.

Scene dock Store for scenery within a theatre.

Scene paint Traditionally, a mixture of glue size, water and pigment. Modern practice has also adopted PVA (emulsion glaze) as a bonding medium which can be used when scenery has not to be washed and used again.

Scene painting Technique involves 'scaling up' from drawings and models to full size. Great skill is necessary in judging colour and texture because the design itself cannot employ scaled-down paint, etc.

Scrim (USA) See *Gauze*: a variety of gauze which is used for bleed throughs.

Script Text of a play.

Season Traditionally the season was the social and West End annual period from autumn to spring during which plays would open and, perhaps, close. Nowadays a season may be of almost any length and in any part of the year.

Section Term in draughtsmanship: see *Elevation*.

Set (a) To place scenery, props etc in position. (b) A set of lines. (c) A complete stage setting for a scene or an act.

Set back Re-set props, scenery, lighting etc, to a point agreed.

Set build Term given to the building of the set onstage.

Setting line A datum line drawn on a ground plan: the point from which setting of scenery starts, usually associated with box sets in proscenium theatres.

Set piece Free-standing or flown, usually three-dimensional scenery such as a staircase or gateway.

Share That part of the box office receipts of a show which belongs to the nominated party in a contract. For example: 40% to the theatre manager (proprietor) and 60% to the *Producer*, from which each pays his overheads and running costs.

Sheave Grooved wheel in a pulley.

Shoe Electrical: two or more socket outlets

in a box or frame on a trailing lead.

Short line Line in a flying set which is nearest to fly floor.

Show (a) Colloquialism for a play, ballet, revue etc. (b) Colloquialism for lowering and raising the safety curtain – 'to show the iron'.

Show report Detailed report giving timings and show information on a performance.

Shutter Metal plate with handle used to shape the beam in a spotlight.

Sightline Or 'line of sight' – hypothetical line on one side of which the audience can see actors, effects, etc, and on the other side of which they cannot.

Sill iron Thin steel sill manufactured specially to fit across the bottom of a door or arch flat to complete its frame but which is nearly invisible to the audience.

Size Glue size – bonding medium in traditional scene paint.

Skip Heavy-duty basket for storage of props and costumes.

Sky cloth Back cloth, painted or plain, used as a sky when lit.

Slap stick Double lath with handle with which clowns beat each other. Derived from Commedia dell'Arte, the tradition sustained to the present day. Gave its name to the sort of humour called *Slapstick*.

Smoke effect See *Pyrotechnics*

Smoke flap Automatically released section of roof or wall to release smoke in case of fire.

Smoke lobby Space between two sets of doors which impedes passage of smoke from one area to another.

Snap Instant – e.g., *Snap blackout* – by switch not fader.

Snap hook Ironmongery fitting otherwise known as a spring hook.

Snap line Chalk covered cord that when pulled tight between two points and snapped on a floor surface it leaves a straight line of chalk.

Snow bag Fabric sewn into a sort of bag, filled with artificial snow, flown out above stage. When hauling lines operated 'snow' falls through slots or holes,

dependent upon type of snow used.

Soliloquy Talking to oneself or without addressing any person.

Sound effect Real or simulated sound, actual or produced by electrical or mechanical means, e.g., gunshot, rain, car etc.

Speech A complete piece of dialogue spoken by an actor to another.

Spigot Metal shaft fitted to the trunnion of a lantern so as to mount it on a stand.

Spike Colloquialism for nailing something.

Spill Stray light.

Splitter Two trailing sockets connected to one plug-top used to supply two separated loads from one channel.

Spot bar Bar or barrel on which spotlights are suspended – usually internally wired for safety and neatness.

Spotlight (a) Lantern with adjustable light beam. (b) Casting directory and advisory service to actors and producers who also publish actors' photographs to aid casting.

Spot line See *Flying*.

Sprinkler Sparge pipe positioned behind the main or house curtain at high level which discharges water in the event of fire – drencher.

Stage May be flat or raked, fitted with machinery or plain. Some types: *Proscenium*: picture frame arch between stage and auditorium through which audience views the play. *End*: similar to proscenium except there is no arch – stage is open to side walls. *In the Round*: acting area encircled by audience. *Transverse*: acting area with audience on either side. *Thrust*: part of stage which projects into auditorium and is partly encircled.

Stage Machinery may include: *Revolve/s*: disc or drum types. *Rolling*: with large sections of floor which move on wheels or rollers. *Lifting*: wholly or partially elevating. *Jack-knife*: where one or two sections of floor pivot at their corner to swing into or out of position for use. *NOTE*: Stage machinery, when installed, is commonly driven by electric motors, wires, chains etc, but in Britain there are some examples of hydraulic equipment.

Stage cloth Heavy canvas or duck cloth, with or without design, which covers the acting area.

Stage directions The physical movements and business of the play as directed, and written into the prompt script.

Stage door Artists' and staff entrance to a theatre.

Stage hand One who sets and strikes scenery.

Stage house (USA) *Fly tower.*

Stage left Actor's left – Prompt side.

Stage main Electrical supply to backstage: separate from front of house and dressing rooms in good practice.

Stage manager Senior member of team, with deputy who usually runs the corner, and assistant stage managers who supervise props, operate sound etc. Also: resident stage manager: senior person in charge backstage.

Stage screw Ironmongery fixing used to fix bottom of extendable brace to stage in theatres which permit holes in floor.

Stage whisper Whispered dialogue between characters in a play which is clearly audible to all members of the audience.

Stand Support for lighting equipment – a sort of rigid tripod.

Star cloth Painted or plain sky cloth to which have been attached miniature electric bulbs which simulate stars.

Stile Vertical member of a flat.

Stillwell An advertisement projector used to show slides on safety curtain or advert-drop: under the terms of a contract with Stillwell Darby who owned the machine and provided theatre programmes free in exchange for the concession to advertise.

Strike Remove scenery, props, equipment etc.

Strobe light Special lamp omitting brilliant blue-white light controlled by a variable pulse circuit. *NOTE*: safety rules apply to avoid inducing epilepsy.

Subscribe State (via Arts Council) or local (Municipal) grant in aid to non-commercial theatre.

Sugar glass Largely superseded by an easily breakable plastic sheet, a substitute for real glass where a breakaway effect is required in a show – frequently seen in Western bar-room brawls in films.

Super See *Extras.*

Swag Arrangement of loops and flutings in draperies on stage.

Tabs Colloquialism for curtains on stage. Derived from tableau, a type of curtain rig in which cords pull through rings on the back of curtains to open them.

Takings Box office receipts.

Tallescope A vertical extending alloy ladder on a wheeled base, topped by a small enclosed working platform just big enough to hold one person. Gives access to onstage lighting bars.

Teaser Border usually black, set behind the proscenium and linked with *Tormentors* to form an inner frame to the stage, and to mask the upper parts of the fly tower.

Thickness piece See *Return.*

Throw Jargon: electrics – in reference to the effective distance a given beam of light will travel.

Throw line (USA) See *Cleat.*

Thrust See *Stage.*

Thunder sheet Steel sheet with handles, suspended on lines, which simulates thunder when rattled.

Tie off Instruction to fix lines when dead is reached: also make off.

Tip-jack Wooden device fitted to offstage side of flat, and wheeled, to assist easy movement of scenery.

Toe See *Run.*

Toggle Horizontal timber brace in construction of a flat.

Top hat Flanged metal tube fitted to front of spotlight to reduce spread of light beam when adjustments have reached their limit.

Top light Vertical beam which is used for effect.

Tormentor Vertical flat on each side of stage – see *Teaser.*

Tour Visit and 'play' in theatres away from 'home'.

Touring date Theatre which receives

touring shows.

Trailing socket Electrics: usually a 15-amp BESA (round pin) socket in a heavy rubber casing.

Train call Details of time to assemble, and departure when using rail on tour – company information.

Transformation Sudden scene change often seen in pantomimes – effected by various methods involving gauzes, folding scenery and lighting.

Trap (a) Manually or mechanically removable section of stage. (b) *Grave, slow and star traps* dating from late 18th century are still found in some theatres and are used for pantomime or in opera. Grave traps are used for 'Hamlet'. Mechanical devices beneath stage are employed to raise or lower actors. When fitted with 'vamps' etc form part of the equipment for real harlequinades.

Travellers Curtains or scenery pieces moving on tracks.

Tread Single or multi-step staircase piece.

Treadmill Form of rolling stage surface which creates the effect of movement in association with diorama.

Traverse Across stage – term usually associated with tab track (curtain track).

Trick line Concealed, or unseen, line of cordage or thread used to operate a trick effect.

Trim (USA) Set borders and bottoms of flown scenery level with stage.

Trip (USA) See *Tumble*.

Tripe Electrics cable feeding a bar which has to be flown to avoid fouling.

Truck Low wheeled platform on which setting (or part setting) may be built to facilitate movement and changes.

Tumble Pick up bottom of cloth with lines to get it out of sight when inadequate height available for flying.

Type casting Casting actors who look and sound like the characters they will play. Casting *against* type is to choose an actor who is not obviously right for the part.

Understudy Actor who takes over another's role in an emergency. A 'walking understudy' has no role in the play but waits in his dressing room for emergencies to occur.

Upstage (a) Toward the back wall. (b) When an actor accidentally or deliberately moves upstage of another and forces the 'victim' to turn away from the audience he is said 'to be upstaging'.

U.V. Abbreviation for ultra violet (black) light. Sometimes used for an effect, sometimes used for staff to work to deads in blackout conditions. Use depends upon the U.V. striking objects or costumes which are inherently, or treated, fluorescent.

Vamp Spring-loaded flaps in scenery or stage floor through which sudden appearances, or disappearances may be made: particularly in traditional harlequinades and pantomimes.

Voice production Vocal technique for power, clarity and conservation of the voice.

Void Empty space in building: e.g., between a circle floor and the ceiling of the stalls beneath it.

Volt Unit of potential difference in electricity.

Vomitory Entrance/exit through banked seating.

Wagon Section of stage which moves on wheels or rollers.

Walk it up Method of raising a flat from the stage floor to the vertical plane.

Walk through A leisurely paced rehearsal of a scene, act or play.

Wardrobe Workroom and store for maintenance of costumes.

Warm up See *Limber*.

Warning Stand by: entered in prompt script in advance of the *Go* cue. In the cue light system *Warnings* are red and gos are green.

Watch your top Instruction to stagehand when running a flat to avoid overhead obstacles such as lines, cables etc.

Watt Unit of electrical power.

Index